THE HOLY SPIRIT
AND OUR FAITH

THE HOLY SPIRIT
AND OUR FAITH

BY J. N. KILDAHL

Revisions by Rolf E. Aaseng
and Grace Gabrielsen

AUGSBURG PUBLISHING HOUSE
MINNEAPOLIS   MINNESOTA

THE HOLY SPIRIT AND OUR FAITH
(Former title *Ten Studies on the Holy Spirit*)
© 1937 and 1960 Augsburg Publishing House

Library of Congress Catalog Card No. 60—12813

Auspices, Department of Parish Education
The American Lutheran Church

Manufactured in the United States of America

Foreword

The greatness of the Christian teacher's task is in the fact that he is involved with more than imparting knowledge or even building attitudes. The Christian teacher is involved with the growth of faith. He is involved with the work of the Holy Spirit in salvation.

Central in the experience of salvation is conversion, turning from sin and self and turning toward repentance and Christ. Such conversion happens to the believer again and again. Sometimes there is a great and decisive turning that changes a man's whole life. Sometimes there are great moments of conversion at the crisis points of life. For every believer there is a continuing series of conversions in the daily renewal of faith and responsible Christian life. Always, in some way, there is a repetition of the Holy Spirit's basic work—to show us our sin and to show us our Savior.

Dr. Kildahl's little classic on the work of the Holy Spirit in salvation speaks again and again of conversion. What is said applies to conversion wherever or however experienced, whether as a first and great turning from self to acceptance of Christ, or as a repeated renewal in the life of a saint. You will find this little book speaking directly to you and your own spiritual situation.

You will also find it speaking to you as a church school teacher, involved in the Spirit's work toward conversions in the lives of your pupils.

This book was first printed in 1927 as *Misconceptions of the Word and Work of the Holy Spirit,* and was later republished as *Ten Studies on the Holy Spirit.* In the present edition, Miss Grace Gabrielsen has added to each chapter a section called "Thoughts of a Church School Teacher." Some suggestions for discussion in leadership training courses are also given at the end of each chapter.

C. RICHARD EVENSON

Contents

Introduction

There is nothing on this earth which is so little understood and so greatly misunderstood as the words and works of the Holy Spirit. "The unspiritual man does not receive the gifts of the Spirit of God, for they are folly to him, and he is not able to understand them because they are spiritually discerned" (I Cor. 2:14). It is really remarkable what a veil covers the eye of the natural man, so that he can neither see nor understand the very simplest things that pertain to the Spirit of God. It matters not how clearly a matter is presented in the Word of God, so long as it is only the natural eye that reads, one will miss the Spirit's meaning. And it matters not how good a natural understanding or comprehension one may have, or how diligently and carefully one has been instructed in the Word of God from childhood, the message of the Spirit is nevertheless hidden, so long as one has not been born again.

In the following chapters we shall consider some of these misconceptions, while we pray to God that what is written may be a help and a blessing to some seeking soul.

THE AUTHOR

Chapter One

Spiritual Awakening

If a worldly-minded person is to repent and believe in the Lord Jesus Christ, it is absolutely necessary that he be awakened. Scripture calls the natural condition of man a sleep and cries out, "Awake, O Sleeper!" So long as a person sleeps in sin, he is not conscious of his true condition. He does not feel his sin, nor is he alarmed about the judgment of God, and he does not seek salvation from sin and judgment. So long as a person sleeps, he does not heed the call of God, but resists the grace offered him, and continues to live without Christ—and therefore without God.

God does not lead sleeping sinners into heaven. An awakening is therefore absolutely necessary. God grant that this may be proclaimed in all our churches, that sleeping sinners may awaken.

What Is Spiritual Awakening?

What constitutes a spiritual awakening? How does it manifest itself? How does it feel to be awakened spiritually? There are many earnest, seeking souls who have a mistaken conception of what a spiritual awakening is. Because they do not understand the Holy Spirit's work in their hearts, they misunderstand their own experiences and resist God's work of grace upon them.

Where God's Word, both Law and Gospel, is preached in its purity, the Holy Spirit is working constantly through this Word to awaken those who are sleeping. Many people have been so influenced by hearing the Word of God preached from week to week that they have begun to feel uneasy about their condition. God's Word has convinced them that all is not well with them, and they go about wishing that their condition might be changed—that they might be converted and live at peace with God.

But they know that if this is to take place they must be spiritually awakened. So they go on waiting for this awakening; but it will not come. They have perhaps heard some person tell of his experiences when he was awakened—how he was so violently gripped that he almost lost his mind. When revival is mentioned they think of it as a mighty shake-up that is likely to come suddenly while they are listening to the Word of God. They have heard of big revivals coming upon whole communities and congregations, where many have been so violently seized by a terrible contrition and grief over sin that they have almost despaired. When they have no such experiences themselves, they do not see how they can be converted and saved; for to them such experiences constitute a spiritual awakening, and must be the way to conversion and salvation.

It must not be denied that many people have had such stirring experiences. There are special periods of visitation by God's Spirit. Sometimes violent revivals come to a whole community; one person after another is mightily seized by the Word. This happened on the day of Pentecost and has also occurred among our congregations today. We rejoice and thank God when people are awakened, no matter how it happens. We also must guard against calling the Spirit's work fanaticism or madness. But this is not the only way in which the Holy Spirit awakens people, and it can scarcely be said to be the most common way.

The fact is that big and violent revivals as a rule are attended by extreme demonstrations and errors bordering on fanaticism. Thus it is of vital importance to distinguish between the works of the Spirit and the imperfect works of man, indiscreet and unsound, that so easily appear.

We must wisely lead the awakened souls, so that they, by God's grace, may be kept from going astray and may be helped to find the right way. On the other hand, we must guard against wanting to dictate to the Holy Spirit certain methods by which He is to awaken and lead sinners to Christ. It is this which characterized the old-time Methodism and gave it its name.

When a man is called by God to repentance, he ought not wait for something extraordinary to happen as though the ordinary call, the ordinary grace, and the ordinary power in the ordinary Word were not sufficient.

The Purpose of Awakening

In order to realize what a spiritual awakening is, it is necessary to have a right understanding of its purpose and aim. The purpose and aim of a spiritual awakening is not to bring a sinner into a spiritual state which so pleases God that because of it He is willing to receive the sinner, bestow upon him faith, and accept him as His child.

Unfortunately, this idea is deeply rooted in the minds of many. They do not believe that God can or will accept them into His grace just as they are. They think that a revival is required to produce a kind of intermediate state which God demands as a condition of being accepted into His grace. This is absolutely wrong and entirely at variance with the Gospel's teaching of salvation by grace through Jesus Christ alone. The purpose and aim of a spiritual awakening is wholly and solely to bring a man to seek salvation and become willing to let God save him.

God earnestly desires to save all men. But so long as a person sleeps in sin, that is, lives in complete indifference in his natural state, God cannot save him, for God cannot save any except those who are willing to be saved. Therefore it is important that the sinner be awakened.

When is he awakened? When he no longer is satisfied with his condition, can no longer live unconcerned about the salvation of his soul, and can no longer be at rest in his old life of sin, but longs to be converted. Then he is spiritually awakened.

This unrest and dissatisfaction with himself and his condition, this longing that a change may take place in him, this desire to have fellowship with God is all brought about by the Holy Spirit. The Spirit's purpose is to induce the sinner to desire to accept grace—to permit the Lord to have him. It is always the Word of God that brings this about.

It may be that the sinner does not at all understand that this very feeling, this restlessness, this desire is the work of the Holy Spirit. But this is in fact the awakening by the Holy Spirit. It may also be that the sinner does not realize that it is the Word of God which has brought it about; for it is not always possible to say at exactly what hour this unrest in the soul began. One cannot always state the hour and place when he began to think more seriously about these things. The impressions may have been made slowly and gradually. Nor is it always possible to name some certain Scripture passage that touched the conscience in a special sense and began the awakening. It may sometimes be the sum total of one's knowledge of Scripture, acquired long ago in childhood, which later begins to work in an individual's conscience because of some event or circumstance in his life.

How Much Awakening Is Needed?

If a person desires to be converted and saved, then he is sufficiently awakened, for grace is free to all who want it. As stated above, a spiritual awakening is necessary to make us willing to accept grace, not in order to induce God to give us His grace. It is a great sin for you to go about imagining that God will not receive you until you are more strongly and intensely awakened. Unbelief lies at the bottom of such thinking.

How intense then must the spiritual awakening be to be sufficient? Since the only aim and purpose of a spiritual awakening is to make the sinner willing to be saved, it is intense enough when the sinner is willing to let God save him. However, it must be so strong, at least, that a sinner no longer will or can find rest in sin and worldliness and uncertainty. It must be so strong that

he cannot find rest in anything but the grace and salvation that are in Christ, and in the assurance in his heart
that he has forgiveness of sins in the blood of Christ.

He who cannot be satisfied with anything less is
spiritually awakened. He who has this need, this desire
or longing in his heart, is spiritually awakened. How he
came to feel such a need and longing, or how this desire
is manifested is of no consequence. The only thing of
importance is this: Do you want to be saved? Do you
desire this so earnestly that you cannot be satisfied with
anything less?

Should you find that this describes your own situation, permit me to say to you: Do you wish to become a
child of God? If you do, then do not go around waiting
for any further awakening. Everything is ready. God
is waiting for you. The way to God is open. Christ has
opened it. "And let him who is thirsty come, let him
who desires take the water of life without price."

THOUGHTS OF A CHURCH SCHOOL TEACHER

Our church schools do not exist for "nice" people. They
are not there only to transmit to a new generation a heritage
of some well-loved Bible stories.

They do not exist to entertain or to serve as a place to
meet friends. They are not there to teach Bible verses or
Catechism, as ends in themselves.

Our church schools exist so that persons may see their
sinfulness and the Christ who died that they may be forgiven, and that believing they may grow in Christian knowledge, faith, and life.

As teachers, we are concerned about the spiritual life of
our pupils. That's why we are teaching. While our basic
spiritual need, that of receiving God's forgiveness, will remain constant throughout life, it will be expressed and ac-

knowledged in different ways at different times. As teachers we need to be aware of this and become sensitive to some of the levels of understanding and experience that can be expected at different periods of life. The preschool child, for example, can think of sin in terms of disobedience and can learn that he needs God's forgiveness for what he has done wrong.

As teachers we also should be conscious of the implications and possible results of some of the things that we say and do. Our words, actions, and attitudes can have a positive effect on an individual pupil's spiritual growth, or a negative one. We can help guide pupils in the right direction, or we can set up road blocks that may hinder the work of the Holy Spirit. By using the wrong words, for example, we can easily lead our pupils to think that they must do something to earn God's love. By an inconsistency between our actions and words, we can confuse or disillusion our students. This might happen, for example, if we talk about forgiveness, but consistently neglect to demonstrate it in dealing with a class member.

As Lutherans, we believe that spiritual life is powerfully related to Holy Baptism. We believe that in Baptism, God adopts the child as His own and gives him the gift of the Holy Spirit.

The baptized child is God's own—a child of God—but he does not know it any more than a newborn child knows he has been given the gift of life. Those who help him to learn, his parents and teachers, have no greater privilege than to help him realize who he is, and what being God's own means for his life. Awakening, for the baptized child, is partly the developing of this conscious awareness of the great truth that God has adopted him as His own and that he belongs to God. This waking up to the great truth that one is a son of God happens over and over again as the individual sees deeper and deeper into the implications that it holds for him.

But even for the baptized child, there is another sense in which he needs to be awakened. For he does not fully understand what this sonship implies and though adopted as God's own, he still possesses a sinful nature. He often rebels against his Heavenly Father. So, daily there is a need for being awakened to his true situation, for acknowledging the need for a Savior. At each age, even the youngest, there is need for an awareness of disobedience and indifference to God, and also for the knowledge that God is loving and forgiving. This need is NOT merely for a more positive relationship with persons in general; the need is for forgiveness from the Heavenly Father!

However, as teachers, we shall also be teaching some pupils who have not been baptized or who have fallen away from their baptismal covenant. Spiritual awakening in these cases involves more exclusively a willingness to acknowledge one's need for God's grace and forgiveness.

In your teaching you will want to be conscious of your unbaptized class members. Baptism must not be seen as merely an initiation rite. It is a means of grace! Occasional references to the gifts that God bestows upon us in Baptism may create in them the desire to be baptized. These gifts include adoption by God as His son, the forgiveness of sin, and deliverance from death and the devil.

Suggestions for Discussion:

1. Do your pupils have an awareness of their need for *forgiveness?*

2. Are your pupils aware of being children of God?

3. What have you understood to be your main purpose in teaching your church school class?

4. What kind of awakening is most needed by members of your class?

A Case to Consider: Luke 15:11-32, The Prodigal Son

(These Bible references are suggested for their illustrative value and because they project positive features that need to be emphasized for a better understanding of each chapter. Because we are constantly failing to see the obvious, the central idea of each chapter should be seen in operation in some familiar Scripture setting. We stand in need of the Word's corrective control lest we stray from the Truth.)

Chapter Two

The Knowledge of Sin

If a sinner is ever to feel the need of grace and have use for Christ and His redemption, he must become conscious of his sin. This is not because the knowledge of sin in itself is prerequisite for grace, or because a knowledge of sin can be exchanged for grace, but simply because "those who are well have no need of a physician, but those who are sick." For even if a person knows ever so much about Christ and knows that it is by faith in Him that we are saved and made eternally happy, still his heart will not desire Christ, nor will he flee to Him, unless he is grieved and troubled because he has learned to know his sin.

The Holy Spirit Reveals Sin

It is the Holy Spirit's work to bring a man to a knowledge of sin, and the means He uses is the Law. "Through the Law comes knowledge of sin" (Rom. 3:20). A person becomes conscious of his sin when, through the work of the Spirit, his eyes are opened to see that his life and condition are in conflict with God's will as revealed in the Law.

The Holy Spirit is the Spirit of truth, that is, He con-

9

vinces people of that which is true. He first tries to
convince them of the truth of their own condition. A
man's realization of his sinfulness is the beginning of
wisdom. Thus, to get people to know and understand
their own sinfulness is the Holy Spirit's work.

Satan has blinded the minds of the unbelieving. The
heart, which is "deceitful above all things," is also seeking to deceive us. So long, therefore, as a man follows
the devil and his own heart, he will live in blindness
and delusion. He will have a false and mistaken opinion
of himself and his own condition. Only by the enlightenment of the Holy Spirit does a person learn to know the
truth about himself. He, therefore, who has come to a
knowledge of sin through the unique work of the Holy
Spirit will have a true and rightful knowledge of his
own condition. What he learns to see in his own heart
is not something imaginary or unreal, but the simple,
naked, and unvarnished truth.

The natural man "does not receive the gifts of the
Spirit of God." That is why he does not understand
what the Holy Spirit is doing when He is trying to
convince him of his sin. The works of the Holy Spirit
are so often misunderstood.

The person who has grown up in a Lutheran congregation has learned that if he is to be converted it is
absolutely necessary that he come to the knowledge of
sin. If there is anything he has heard ever since childhood it is this. Therefore, if such a person is spiritually
awakened, that is, becomes concerned about the salvation of his soul and begins to desire to be converted,
he will also desire to come to the knowledge of sin, for
he knows that this is the way he must go to be saved.

But the Holy Spirit may be striving to bring him to a

thorough knowledge of his deep corruption and spiritual wretchedness, his great fall and utter depravity, without his understanding that this is just what he feels and experiences in his heart. He goes about hoping he may become truly humble, contrite, and penitent; but instead he feels frightfully hard and impenitent. He knows he ought to just melt away in a deep feeling of penitence, but instead he feels an alarming coldness and lack of earnestness. He knows he ought to pray with more intensity, but instead he notices he is not able to put any warmth or intensity into his prayers. He thinks he ought seriously to pull himself together, force his way to God, and take the Kingdom of Heaven unto himself by force; but instead he finds that he cannot move from the spot where he is. He feels he is far away from God and is not even able to begin with the first step of conversion, which to be sure ought to be remorse and contrition for sin. And because he cannot bring any of this to pass, it seems impossible for him ever to be converted. How can he appear before God when he cannot even begin to feel a true and thorough consciousness of his sin?

Let us consider this more closely. If the knowledge of sin is to be real and true, it seems that what one sees and feels within himself ought to correspond to the description of the natural condition of a sinner found in the Word of God. Therefore he who sees himself as the Word of God has described the natural condition of the heart of man has a true and thorough knowledge of his sin.

But sin does not consist primarily of certain sinful deeds, words, and thoughts. It consists chiefly and particularly in an inward depravity, an utter lack of love for God, fear of God, and trust in God. Instead there is a constant inclination to the things that conflict with the will and command of God. The natural man's condition is the direct opposite of what it ought to be; in addition, the natural man finds that he has not the slightest power or strength to change or correct this condition.

Man Has a Heart of Stone

How is the natural man's heart described in the Word of God? It is described as a *heart of stone*. If therefore a man gets a true knowledge of his own heart, what does he discover? Does he find that his heart is humble, tender, and easily moved? Does he find that his heart just melts away in contrition, devotion, and submission to the will of God? No, one who permits the Holy Spirit, the Spirit of truth, to lead him to a knowledge of sin—a true and correct knowledge of his real condition—finds only a heart of stone.

Now surely it is not strange if he finds and feels that a heart of stone is hard, cold, unyielding, and unreceptive. One who is distressed about his heart being so hard and cold and impenitent, who complains that he cannot make it tender, warm, and humble, has begun to see himself *just as he is,* and just as the Word of God says he is. He has therefore begun to acquire a *thorough* knowledge of his sin. But it is self-evident that such consciousness of sin is not a pleasant feeling which one can enjoy because he thinks that now everything connected with his conversion is proceeding very well. Instead it is a very unpleasant and disheartening feeling which leaves him not knowing what to do.

The knowledge of sin may, it is true, begin by having

one's eyes opened to certain definite sins, and by becoming distressed and terrified at them. But so long as the knowledge of sin stops at certain outward expressions of sin it is a very superficial knowledge. It is not thorough until it achieves a feeling and understanding of the evil, hard, cold, perverted, godless, obstinate, deceitful, and unbelieving heart of stone, which is unwilling and incapable of doing anything good.

It is when a person begins to examine this evil heart that he bcomes really perplexed and puzzled. When he begins to probe into this heart; and perhaps through the convincing work of the good Spirit gradually learns to know it more and more fully, he feels anything but repentant; he believes anything but that he is coming to the knowledge of sin. The trouble is that he has the mistaken idea that when God began His work in him he should have felt and perceived something godly taking place in his heart. When instead of this he only feels ungodly, he cannot believe that what he feels and perceives is the work of the Holy Spirit. So the work of the Holy Spirit is misunderstood.

Neither does he think that he can begin to believe in Christ so long as he feels this way. Much persuasion is required before the sinner believes the blessed truth that God justifies the *ungodly.* There is nothing that is so strange, remote, and hidden to the natural man as this truth, that we must be saved just as we are; or in other words, that we are saved by grace.

If there should be anyone reading this who recognizes how hard and wicked and ungodly he is inwardly, and who is waiting to become better before he can begin to believe, then let me say: Your condition will not be improved in all eternity so long as you will not begin to believe in Christ. If you are to be saved, you must permit God to save you in your present wicked and ungodly condition. He never saves any other kind of people. Believe in the Lord Jesus Christ, and you shall be saved.

THOUGHTS OF A CHURCH SCHOOL TEACHER

The chances are it took us many, many years, and many fierce battles within our soul to come to the conclusion that "sin does not consist primarily of certain sinful deeds, words, and thoughts. It consists chiefly and particularly in an inward depravity, an utter lack of love for God, fear of God, and trust in God. Instead there is a constant inclination to the things that conflict with the will and command of God." Since this is an adult concept of sin, we cannot expect little children to come to this conclusion quickly. They are simply not ready to think in such abstract terms.

The child is not very old when he realizes that certain things he does seem to meet with mother's approval and some of his other activities are frowned upon. This is a matter of important concern for him. He needs mother's approval and tries to discover what he can do to retain this approval. This is not always easy to do. Certain actions are acceptable in one kind of situation but not in another.

But the real standard of right and wrong at this preschool age level remains mother or teacher. For the preschooler, and even the first and second grader, our task as teachers should be to help the child understand that *God* says there are things that we should do and things that we should not do. In specific instances these can be equated with what mother or teacher tell us to do. A child knows that he is disobedient and needs to be reassured that God loves him even when he does things that are wrong.

First and second graders have recently found themselves in a competitive school situation. They must, for example, learn to read—by themselves. Part of teacher's approval depends on it. Parents show obvious interest and concern as to whether or not this is happening. The child may begin to fear that he will lose their love if he doesn't learn. He may begin to think of God in the same way and fear that "God won't love me if I'm naughty." It is important, therefore, for the teacher to assure the child of the constancy of God's love —even when he's bad.

Somewhere around third or fourth grade, concepts of right and wrong become very important. The child can understand a generalization such as "Thou shalt not steal," and can perhaps begin to apply it in new situations. At this stage, the child is still thinking of sin as specific acts that are sinful. He thinks in terms of sins, not in terms of sin. The teacher can be of great help to his pupils in helping them think through some of these situations. The child, through the junior years, may want to think of right and wrong as being as clearly distinguished as black and white. The teacher can help him to see that there are also shades of gray.

Through these years the gang may play an important part in the life of the child, and exert influence on his judgments of right and wrong. He may try to justify himself by thinking that "everybody does it." The teacher can help here in guiding him to realize that people keep changing their ideas of what is acceptable, but God has set up an absolute, unchanging standard of right and wrong.

Teen-agers have a keen sense of justice and fairness and look for these qualities, or their absence, in actions of their superiors. But at the same time they can be overwhelmed with a sense of their own personal guilt.

It is probably during the teen years that some individuals come to the realization that sin lies not so much in the act as in the individual. This is a difficult thing to acknowledge, and many individuals never reach this point. The Pharisees in Jesus' day, for example, preferred to think in terms of specific rules and observances. Our own day is not without its Pharisees.

It is a much more comfortable way of thinking and living. Somehow we feel more in control of the situation, since we determine what we do and do not do and therefore feel that we can refrain from doing certain things if we really want to. The knowledge of sin does not consist of admitting to a sinful act. It consists rather of a deep and painful acknowl-edgement of a state of sinfulness—against which we are unsuccessful in our battle. All we can do is cry to God for mercy.

At all stages of growth the teacher will be aware that the spiritual maturity toward which the child is growing involves such a knowledge of sin.

Suggestions for Discussion:

1. What concepts of sin are held by members of your class?

2. What indications of mistaken ideas about sin have you noticed in the conversation and actions of your class mem-bers?

3. Can you think of times when your class has become more conscious of the reality of sin?

A Case to Consider: Psalm 32; Isaiah 6,
The Effects of Sin

Chapter Three

The Purpose of the Law

One who has been brought up in a Lutheran congregation, who has been instructed in the Catechism, who is confirmed, and who has heard Christian sermons, knows that the Law must do its work in a man's heart before he can believe in Christ. He knows it is the Law which the Holy Spirit uses to bring forth sorrow for sin, that the knowledge of sin comes by the Law, and that the Law is our tutor to bring us to Christ.

That the Law must accomplish its work in the heart of a man who is to believe in Christ is quite true. But there are, unfortunately, many mistaken notions of just what the Law is to accomplish in the heart. Since the Law is good, many are of the opinion that what is brought forth as a fruit of the work of the Law upon one must also be good. In fact they think it is so good and pleasing to God that because of it He is willing to accept them into His grace. However, it is a big mistake to believe that the Law is capable of bringing forth anything good in the heart of an unconverted person.

The Law Becomes Serious

When a man is spiritually awakened, that is, begins to reflect seriously, he will no longer despise the Law

17

nor treat it with deadly indifference. On the contrary, he will begin to understand that it is a serious matter to persist in living a sinful life, and he will begin to heed the will of God. A sure sign that he has become serious is that he has begun to strive to live according to the Law and to become as God wants him to be, both in his life and inwardly in his soul, his heart, and his nature. And this, to be sure, is entirely right.

But now, when he begins seriously to strive to obey the Law, what is the result? Will he really become better, more humble, more earnest, more tender, and more godly? That is what you might expect. Since the Law is good, and the sinner is now earnestly striving to become what the Law demands he should be, one might think that he will become better as a result. But one who believes this does not know himself or how he is constituted, and does not know what the depravity of the natural man really is.

The Law Makes One Worse

On the contrary, the result of trying to keep the Law is that one becomes worse. He not only feels worse, being more conscious of his sin, he really does become worse. Sin really does become more abundant. So evil and utterly corrupt is human nature, that far from becoming more pious and worthy of esteem when the good and holy Law comes to a person with its demands, it is on the contrary goaded to become more wicked and ungodly.

It is not the Law which causes the sin in the heart, for that which is good cannot be the cause of something evil. Rather it is sin or the evil nature in man which is goaded on by the Law, and which takes advantage of it to work evil in the heart. This is clearly and distinctly taught in the seventh chapter of Romans. "But sin, finding opportunity in the commandment," says Paul, "wrought in me all kinds of covetousness. Apart from the law sin lies dead . . . when the commandment came, sin revived and I died; the very commandment which promised life proved to be death to me. For sin, finding opportunity in the commandment, deceived me and by it killed me. . . . Did that which is good, then [i.e., the Law], bring death to me? By no means! It was sin, working death in me through what is good, in order that sin might be shown to be sin, and through the commandment might become sinful beyond measure."

This is exactly what so many discover, to their great surprise and dismay, when they are spiritually awakened. They have lived an ungodly life without being concerned about the will of God. Now they have become serious; they want to quit this godless life, forsake the service of sin, and return to God. They begin by striving to heed God's will, conform to His commands, and obey Him. But they discover that instead of becoming better, they actually become worse.

They can desist from openly transgressing God's commands, e.g., against cursing or stealing. But if they have been instructed in the Word of God they know that this is not enough. An inward change is required. This change, *they think*, is performed partly by the Law, and partly by the Gospel. They think that first the Law must humble them and make them penitent and yielding. When it has accomplished this work and so made them qualified for grace, the Gospel will make them children of God, grant them faith, and lead them into a blessed fellowship with God.

But their experience, as already pointed out, is that the Law does not seem to help them become more humble and worthy, and thus more deserving of grace; on the contrary they become more sinful and unworthy. "I was once alive apart from the Law," says Paul in the aforementioned chapter of Romans, "but when the commandment came, sin revived."

As long as one lives apart from the Law and is indifferent to it, he is scarcely aware of the depravity in his own heart. Consequently unconverted people can believe that they have a good heart, as we sometimes hear them say. But just let loose the Law with its holy demands on the heart and see what happens. Then the old Adam rises up. He cannot endure holiness pressing in upon him; he is provoked by the Law and rises up to resist it.

The wicked heart may be likened to a vicious, evil-tempered dog. He may lie there quite still and may seem ever so good-natured and harmless so long as no one comes too near. But if anyone approaches him, immediately the hairs on his back begin to bristle and he shows his teeth. The natural man is just like this in relation to the Law. Therefore Paul says in the eighth chapter of Romans that the Law is "weakened by the flesh." It is incapable of bringing forth anything good in the heart. It matters not how good the Law may be; what it is dealing with is so evil and corrupt that it becomes entirely powerless.

If the foregoing is true, we can understand how useless it is to try to use the Law to change ourselves in a good way; and how impossible it is to bring forth in the heart anything godly and acceptable unto God by the help of the Law.

The Purpose of the Law

No, the work which the Law is to perform in the heart of a sinner before he can believe in Christ and accept His grace is of quite a different nature; it has another purpose.

What is it then that the Law must accomplish in us before we can accept His grace? Let us remember that God never offers His grace to anyone on certain conditions. That would be contrary to the nature and character of grace. Grace is absolutely free. Whoever wants grace gets it. But there is only one class of people who will let God prevail upon them to accept His grace. These are the ones who will let themselves be convinced by the Word of God that if they are ever to be saved, they must be saved as *ungodly* persons, and not as people who once may have been ungodly but now, by God's help, have become a little better so God can accept them into His grace.

The office of the Law is therefore to *shut our mouths* and make us *guilty before God* (Rom. 3:19). In other words, the work of the Law is to convince us so thoroughly of our utter depravity, incapacity, lack of power, and spiritual death that we have nothing more to say, either as an excuse or in our defense. We can only stand before Him fully acknowledging and confessing ourselves guilty. The work of the Law is to make us so bankrupt and destitute, so hopeless and perplexed that we entirely give up the thought and hope that our condition can and will be improved before God can accept us into His grace. It is the purpose and work of the Law to make us lost and condemned sinners who are absolutely incapable of doing anything, who can see only this one thing, that we are sinners and nothing but sinners.

Not till then is it possible to teach anyone what it means to be *saved by grace*. Not till then is one willing to be saved in the only way that God saves sinners—which after all is the only possible way by which sinners can be saved—namely, by grace.

There is nothing so humiliating and so hard for our proud and self-righteous natures as just this. But if only the Law with its inexorable demands for holiness and perfection is let loose upon us, if we but begin to take the words of the Law in real earnest, then will the Law crush our pride, and so thoroughly lash and beat us that we shall begin to plead for grace—only grace, grace. Then we are saved, for then we are saved by grace.

THOUGHTS OF A CHURCH SCHOOL TEACHER

The purpose of the Law is first and foremost to show us our sin and our need for a Savior.

Too often we have tended to use the Law for quite a different purpose. We have often tried to use it as a guide so that we would be better people, living better lives. We have, for example, looked at the Fifth Commandment, "Thou shalt not kill." Our pupils may look at this commandment and think they have done pretty well in observing it. Since we want them to obey it on a deeper level, we show them Jesus' interpretation of it in the Sermon on the Mount. Here they see the relationship of this commandment to things such as anger and hatred. We think that by so doing we are educating our pupils "not to sin." When we are realistic, we realize that such knowledge does not really help them to be better.

While the teacher may think that he is helping his students to live better lives through this teaching and exposition of the Law, he may unintentionally lead them to some false conclusions. It is very easy when talking about the need for obeying the Law to begin to think that we can please God by what we do. This is in direct contrast to the primary purpose of the Law—to show us that we cannot in ourselves please God, but that we need the forgiveness offered to us in Christ.

In our teaching of the Law we want our pupils to realize that just as we do not become children of God by obeying the commandments, God does not reject us as His children because we break them. We are justified by faith, not by works, lest any man should boast. But even though, through Christ, we are just in the sight of God, we do retain our old sinful nature and are in need of forgiveness—daily.

Teaching the Law is a basic part of the work of the teacher, for it is indeed the Law that makes us see our need for Christ. But the Law must not be seen merely as a set of rules to which we conform. It is in the great commandment, "You shall love the Lord your God with all your heart, and with all your soul, and with all your mind . . . and . . . your neighbor as yourself" (Matt. 22:37-39), that we see the essence of the Law. And in the life of Christ we see this "law of love" fulfilled.

As teachers we are not true to our calling if we add our own personal prejudices or legalistic ideas to the Law. We must rather help our students to interpret the Law in the light of the great commandment and the present day situation so that the Holy Spirit may convict them of their sin and help them see their need of the Savior.

Suggestions for Discussion:

1. Can you think of times when you have misled pupils by adding your own personal prejudices to what the Law of God says?

2. Evaluate the following statements in the light of the purpose of the Law:

   a. The commandments tell us what God wants us to do.

   b. If we know what God expects, then we can really become Christians.

3. Can you pick out some basic points of view on the Law as to

   a. why we should obey the Law—
      (because God commands it? so we can get along better?)

   b. what the Law says—
      (be perfect? be nice?)

   c. what the Law does for us—
      (shows us our sin? shows us the way to be saved?)

A Case to Consider:

Luke 18:9-14, The Pharisee and the Publican

Chapter Four

Works of the Law

"For no human being will be justified in his sight by
works of the Law" (Rom. 3:20). If there is anything
which Lutheran church people have heard, it is this.
And if there is anything that Lutheran church people
look upon as divine truth, it is this. But if there is anything which no unconverted person understands, it is
this same truth. And if there is anything which every
single grown person who has been spiritually awakened
will try, it is to be justified by works of the Law.

The natural man does not grasp the things of the
Spirit of God. The natural man's religion is that one
is accepted into grace by God because of what he himself is or does. And so long as one is only a natural man,
that is, so long as he is not born of God, he has the
natural religion. That he has acquired a historical
knowledge of Christianity does not alter the matter.
The only difference is that a person who has been instructed in the Word of God uses Christian words and
expressions, but he puts into these words and expressions the meaning of the natural religion.

He therefore misunderstands the words of the Holy
Spirit, and consequently misunderstands the Spirit's
works as well. The fact that he has learned by heart

that man is justified alone by faith in Christ, and admits this to be true, does not change anything. He does not understand what these words mean; in fact, he cannot understand them for they are "spiritually discerned." The fundamental condition for understanding the essentials of Christianity is lacking in one who is not born of God (or, if baptized, has become so undernourished spiritually that his only effective life is really that of the "natural man").

Natural Religion Is a Religion of Law

Therefore it does not matter what an unconverted person professes and thinks he believes; the only religion which he understands and therefore has is the religion of the works of the Law. Of course he will not admit this, but will insist, very emphatically maybe, that he believes what Paul teaches concerning the matter—until he himself is converted. Then he will see that he never before understood what it means to be justified by faith.

A person who has been brought up in a Lutheran congregation understands that one who has transgressed God's commands and has lived a life in sin away from the Lord will not be justified and saved by doing some outward works, such as donating money to the Church or being charitable to the poor. He knows that Christianity is of a more spiritual nature. Consequently he is not living in the grossest form of work-righteousness. And yet all experience shows us that all unconverted persons, so far as their struggle to win God's favor is concerned, are in the toils of self-righteousness. This is clearly brought to light when they are awakened.

What is it that people who have been awakened to a solicitude for the salvation of their souls first think of and first strive to do? Is it to believe in Christ? Believe in Christ—at the very start? No. They hope to come to it some day; but they have not yet reached that point in the way of salvation. Something else is required first, they think. So they continue with the works of the Law, hoping by this means to arrive at a point where they can begin to believe.

They themselves do not believe that they are struggling with the works of the Law, but that is the case, nevertheless. Let one who has been awakened from his sleep in sin open his heart and tell us just what he is troubled about, what kind of thoughts he harbors in his heart, what burden is oppressing him. We shall see that it is the heavy service of the Law, insisted on by self-righteousness, with which he is struggling as best he can. He has been disturbed in his life of sin. He sees that things will go from bad to worse if he continues in the old way; there must be a change. He resolves to return to God and become His child.

But he cannot make it work. He is growing worse rather than better, going backward rather than forward to God. And he sighs, "Oh, if only I could become truly earnest; if only I could pray with more fervor; if only I could truly humble myself before God so He could exalt me! If only I were not so cold, so hard, so impenitent!"

But let me ask this person, do you not believe that a person is justified and saved by faith alone, apart from the works of the Law? "Yes, of course I believe that, but. . . ." If you believe that, why are you so concerned about all these other things you mentioned?" Concerned?

Why, doesn't God require them of us? Must we not become truly earnest, must we not humble ourselves before God if we are to be exalted by Him?"

What is implied in this apparently reasonable talk? Simply this: *the sinner first wants to find in himself something which will give him at least a little comfort before he feels he is permitted to find comfort in Jesus and what He has done.* It wouldn't be quite so discouraging if he ever could find in his own heart what he is trying so hard to work up there. Actually what he is trying to find comfort in is an assurance that inwardly, in his own soul and heart, he is so constituted that God can find enough pleasure in him to begin to convert him. He wants to be assured that God no longer looks upon him as one who is only hard, cold, obstinate, and impenitent, but as one who is fit to be pardoned.

But isn't it just such an inward condition that the first commandment of the Law requires of us? Therefore, what you are striving to do are actually works of the Law; they are the inward works which are required in the first commandment. You think you must have these works. And what do you want of them? Well, you want to display them, as it were, before God, and then you would think: surely now God will find enough pleasure in me so that He will be willing to grant me faith, regenerate me, and accept me as His child.

Don't you understand that this is not seeking salvation *alone* by faith in Jesus, but is clinging to the works of the Law? You think that you do not want to reject Christ and the doctrine of salvation by faith in Him. But what you really want, whether you understand it or not, is to be saved partly by the works of the Law and partly by faith in Christ. You hope that the works of the

Law will get you part way, and that God will meet you there with Christ and lead you the rest of the way to heaven. By your works of the Law you hope to become prepared and fit to receive faith so that then by faith you may receive salvation.

However, "works of the Law" means all that a person does or is in harmony with the Law. By works of the Law is meant not only outward works, but also, and chiefly, such an inward condition of the heart as harmonizes with the first commandment. It is this state which you think God demands as a condition for grace. This is not true.

God Never Trades Grace

God never trades His grace for anything He finds in the heart of man, whether one thinks of this as something man has brought about by his own strength or has cultivated in his heart by God's help, or as something which God alone, without our help, has created and brought forth. Grace is only *given* away, and grace is given only to those who are ungodly, unworthy, and lost. For "if it is by grace, it is no longer on the basis of works; *otherwise grace would no longer be grace*" (Rom. 11:6).

So long as a person imagines that God requires something which must be worked up in the heart as a condition for giving grace, just so long does he hold fast to the Law, continuing with works of the Law, lying bound in self-righteousness and work-righteousness, resisting grace and the Gospel, and hindering the Holy Spirit from doing His work in his heart.

Therefore no one is converted to God before his own

self-made conversion goes entirely to pieces and he stands before God naked and unclothed. "For no human being will be justified by works of the Law," neither by inward nor by outward works of the Law; neither by works according to the second table of the Law, nor by works according to the first table; neither by anything which one does, nor by anything which one is—not by any condition to be found in the heart or soul.

For that gate is narrow; it is so narrow that no man carrying a pack can get through it; it is so narrow that the only way to get through it is to be entirely unclothed. All that a person strives to do because he thinks it ought to belong to a true conversion and that God demands it—these things are works of the Law. So long as he doesn't believe that God accepts him into His grace as poor, miserable, ungodly, and lost—as he is— just so long is he clinging to the works of the Law.

And since there is no power or ability in the soul to do any of the works of the Law before faith is kindled in the heart, or in any way to bring forth something pleasing to God, all such work is entirely in vain and brings no one a hair's breadth nearer to God. The corruption of the soul is so great, the incapacity is so complete, that this is just what one is incapable of doing. There will be absolutely nothing else than death and damnation in such work; for all who rely on works of the Law are under a curse (Gal. 3:10).

The only way to escape the curse is to believe that Scripture tells the truth when it says that "to one who does not work but trusts him who justifies the ungodly, his faith is reckoned as righteousness" (Rom. 4:5).

THOUGHTS OF A CHURCH SCHOOL TEACHER

"That's a good boy!" "I'm a good girl aren't I, Mommy?" How often haven't you heard statements like this. We all seem to have this desire to be "good." Being good seems to mean that we have the approval of other people, that we can do pretty well ourselves, and that we don't need any help.

We grow up with some of these ideas from toddlerhood on. The toddler is good when he eats his vegetables. He's good when he goes right to sleep at nap time. The child soon learns that it is more comfortable to be good than to be bad.

The child in school learns that he should be good. He learns that there are rewards that come to him when he is good, and punishments that come to him when he is not. Trying to please people and trying to please God by what we do come quite naturally to us.

Even as adults, we strive to be good to avoid possible punishment. We do, for example, stop for the traffic light late at night when there are no cars at all in the neighborhood. Our whole culture seems to be based on this idea, that we strive to be good to meet the approval of certain groups or persons, or to avoid displeasing others who might reprove or punish us. It is not surprising then to realize that we and our students do have tremendous difficulty in trying to understand that in the sight of God we cannot be justified by our own works. "Being good" has always worked in relation to our fellow man so that this is what we now try to do in relation to the Holy God.

The only difference is that here it doesn't work!

We can *never* meet the perfect standard of the Holy God! There is a difference between loving the Lord your God with all your heart, soul, and mind and your neighbor as yourself, and stopping for red lights, voting at the right times, paying taxes, and refraining from robbing banks.

As teachers, we must be very careful to avoid reinforcing the idea that we can gain merit before God through what we do. For this our pupils will try to do! This is natural religion. This is a religion of law. "For the word of the cross is folly to those who are perishing, but to us who are being saved it is the power of God" (I Cor. 1:18). Our pupils must come to realize that the Word of the cross is not folly, but absolutely necessary, since they cannot in themselves satisfy the demands of God. A totally new and different answer must be found. The Gospel supplies this answer.

As Christians we are freed from the curse of the Law. We do not have to strive to obey God's Law in order to please Him or to earn our salvation.

In Holy Baptism we have received spiritual regeneration and we have, in very fact, not only the natural man, but also the new man within us. The new man has seen and experienced God's goodness, love, and forgiveness. In a response of thankfulness, we *desire* to serve God and do what will be pleasing in His sight.

It is important that the teacher distinguish between works of the Law done in an attempt to earn salvation, and the response to grace done to express thankfulness and love.

Suggestions for Discussion:

1. Each generation has its own peculiar forms of legalism. Many religious people place great emphasis on following the mode—and think they are therefore Christian. Once it was "don't dance, wear make-up, or play cards." Or, "don't smoke or drink." Or, "don't be a non-participant, but belong to good organizations." What do you think is the current form of legalism that might mislead your pupils? (Just listen to their definition of "What is a Christian?")

2. Conduct a little research at this point. Ask your pupils next Sunday, "What is a Christian?" If they are above the fifth or sixth grades, have them write their answers. Do not begin correcting or discussing their answers until all have responded. Report their answers exactly and discuss these answers at the next teachers' meeting. They are a clue to the concepts held by your pupils.

A Case to Consider:
Mark 10:17-22, The Rich Young Ruler

Chapter Five

The Gospel

The natural man understands *something* about the
Law, but absolutely nothing about the Gospel. The
Gospel is the big mystery; it has never entered into the
heart of man, and no natural man has or ever can have
any conception of it.

The Gospel Is Unique

The Gospel is something which is peculiar to the
Christian religion. Law is found in all religions; but
Christianity is the only religion in the world which con-
tains anything like the Gospel. If all the wise men of
the world had together racked their brains they would
never have thought of anything like the Gospel. Nothing is so strange and remote from the thoughts of the
natural man as the Gospel.

This is not because the Gospel in itself is so intricate,
lofty, or difficult to understand. Nothing is more simple
and straightforward than the Gospel. Many a person who
for a long time had been fumbling in the dark has been
quite surprised, when his eyes were opened, that it was
so simple and that he had not seen this before. But
this is because the Gospel lies in a sphere which the

33

natural man with his understanding cannot reach.

The fact is that the natural man is blind to things concerning the Spirit of God, and as we all know, a blind man does not see even the things that are clear as noon-day. Even if the Gospel is preached, yes, explained ever so clearly and distinctly, and if the one to whom it is explained has ever so keen a mind and ever so good an apprehension, still he does not understand the Gospel before God has opened his eye in the new birth. Therefore the Gospel is to the Jews a stumbling block and unto the Greeks foolishness. And it is, as said before, a hidden mystery to all natural men.

People who have learned Luther's Catechism know that it is correct teaching to say that man is saved not by the Law but by the Gospel. But it does not make any difference how well a person has been instructed, the natural man still does not understand what the Gospel is and therefore does not know what it means to be saved by the Gospel.

It Is Natural to Make the Gospel a Law

All unregenerate persons make the Gospel over into Law. The only thing they do understand somewhat is the Law, and when they hear and think of the Gospel they think of it in terms of the Law. The Law is so deeply rooted in their heads and hearts that they cannot get away from it. The characteristic thing about the Law is that it promises eternal life on certain conditions which we must meet. The characteristic thing about the Gospel is that it promises eternal life as a free gift of grace.

But when the natural man begins to concern himself

with the Gospel, he brings along the characteristic of
the Law into his reflections about the Gospel. All
natural persons, that is, all unregenerate persons, look
upon the Gospel as something that promises eternal life
on certain conditions. When therefore God the Holy
Spirit calls them by the Gospel and through the Gospel
offers them free grace, they do not understand this
language. And when the Holy Spirit is trying to create
faith in their hearts they misunderstand His work, resist
His operations, and so hinder the birth of the new life
in their hearts.

People who have been spiritually awakened and
earnestly desire to be converted are not aware of the
fact that they do not understand what the Gospel is
and that they are resisting the work of grace in their
hearts. Nevertheless, this is the case so long as they are
not willing to believe.

There are only two conceivable ways of coming to
God, by the Law and by the Gospel. The way of the
Law is: "Do this and you shall live." The Gospel says,
"Believe, and you shall be saved." Faith is the first step
on the way of the Gospel. Faith is not something to
which the Gospel eventually leads after it has performed a great deal of preparatory work in the heart.
One must *begin* by believing. The Gospel is not an offer
of grace, salvation, forgiveness, and sonship on certain
conditions which, "by God's help," we are to fulfill. It
does not require as a stipulation for grace any state or
condition in the one to whom it comes. It is the Law
which is engaged in such work.

The Gospel is simply a historical account of what
God has done in and through Christ, a story of what
took place in Judea nineteen hundred years ago. It is

simply an account which shows that we are a redeemed
people. It tells something which is true, and therefore
must be believed. And this same Gospel tells us that
he who believes what is proclaimed in the Gospel shall
receive the forgiveness of sins and shall be saved. There
is absolutely no condition of any kind, no demands or
requirements as to the condition of the heart or soul in
those to whom these free tidings come. The Gospel
only relates a historical fact and says, "Believe this and
you shall be saved."

How often has not a pastor, trying to lead spiritually
awakened people to Christ, had the experience that all
their thoughts were turned to the condition of their own
hearts, so that he could not get them to look to Christ
and His atonement. He tries his best to hold the crucified Christ before the troubled sinner, and explains as
simply and clearly as possible that Christ has redeemed
him, that all things are ready, and that he only has to
believe in Jesus. And the poor, perplexed sinner sits
there staring into space without understanding, but
answers to all he hears: "Yes, I believe all, but . . .
but . . . but." And what is this objection which is always
obscuring the cross of Christ so that a person cannot see
himself as a saved sinner? It is that I—I—I am not what
I ought to be.

What does this show? It shows that this person does
not yet understand at all what the Gospel is. He is
bound by the Law. It is the Law which is always telling
how I ought to be. The Gospel never speaks of how I
ought to be. It tells only of Him, *Him*, HIM. It says,
"Behold the Lamb of God who takes away the sin of
the world!"

Oh, if only the Gospel could persuade you to look

away from yourself, both from your sin and your hard, wicked heart, and from what you hope by God's help to accomplish, and only look at Jesus and listen to what He has done! Then would the daystar arise in your heart, and you would sing praises to God for the salvation you found fully prepared in Christ.

What Preparation Is Required?

But is not a preparation of the heart required before the Gospel can do this work in us? So long as a person lives in levity, thoughtlessness, and impenitence, and only seeks the things of this world, he cares nothing for the grace which is freely offered in the Gospel. Therefore God must by means of the Law bring about such a condition in the heart that he feels it is hard to be a sinner, and desires to get out of this state and be saved. Those who are well have no need of a physician, but only those who are sick.

What preparation is required before seeking a doctor? Simply this: one must feel that he needs medical attention. So it is here. He who feels that he is a sinner, who understands that it is no joke to have transgressed God's commands, and who therefore earnestly desires to find grace and salvation—for such a one there is grace. "The grace of God has appeared for the salvation of *all* men," and there is no conditional clause in the Gospel. Those who are sent out to invite men to the feast of grace have been instructed to say to everyone—as many as they find—"Come, for all is now ready." And on the last page of the Bible is written, "And let him who is thirsty come, let him who desires take the water of life without price." No preparation of the heart is required to induce

God to give us His grace; for as previously stated, grace is something which one cannot get by bartering any kind of preparation whatever for it. It is given away only to the unworthy.

But often a great deal of preparation is required to induce us to accept that grace which is offered us unconditionally in the Gospel, entirely without price. Enough preparation is required to make us so utterly destitute, bankrupt, and perplexed that we at last are willing to be saved just as we are. A preparation is therefore required not for God's sake but for our sake. If one desires to escape from sin and wants God to have mercy on him, he is sufficiently prepared. The longer he waits before he is willing to accept grace, the more miserable will he become.

We have accounts in the Gospels of many people who were different in some respects; but all were alike in this, that they were in trouble and needed help. They had heard that Jesus could and would help them, and they in their helplessness came to Him. Do we read in a single instance of Jesus saying to any of them, "Yes there is enough grace and help and salvation to be had with me, but you are coming too soon. You are not earnest enough, not penitent enough, not contrite enough; you must first go home and bring about a more thorough penitence and preparation. Then you can come back again, and we shall see what can be done"? No, it never happened and it never will happen; He received all who came; they were welcomed heartily. And He says, "Him who comes to me, I will not cast out." This is Gospel.

THOUGHTS OF A CHURCH SCHOOL TEACHER

In this chapter you read: "The Gospel is simply a historical account of what God has done in and through Christ,
a story of what took place in Judea nineteen hundred years
ago. . . . The Gospel only relates a historical fact and says,
'Believe this, and you shall be saved.'" There are no conditions; there are no strings attached.

Martin Luther, in the Explanation to the Third Article of
the Creed, says that the "Holy Spirit calls me through the
Gospel." This story is the instrument that God uses to tell
me of His love for me.

The Gospel is the instrument that God uses to tell *my children* of His love for them. It simply says, "Believe this proc-
lamation of God's love and you shall be saved."

As teachers there is a danger against which we must guard.
This involves turning the Gospel into a new law, or placing
conditions on God's forgiveness. Often we do this when we
unintentionally preface the Gospel message with an "if"
thereby placing a condition on God. For example we might
say, "*if* we repent and believe, God will forgive us." What
we are saying in such a statement is that God cannot act until we have acted. This is not so.

Rather, God offers us forgiveness in Christ. We are free to
accept it, or free to reject it.

By way of contrast to this simple message of the Gospel
let's look at some stories that are sometimes used in Sunday
school or in various kinds of religious literature. you will
want to be very critical in your evaluation of these. Check
carefully the

—"experience" stories and illustrations you have used
in your lessons;

—the stories in your Sunday school papers and lesson
materials;

—the content of the material in any religious books
you buy, or give, or use.

Read these critically and ask yourself these questions in
connection with them:

1) Will your children judge themselves in the light of a standard set by the fictional child rather than in the light of God's perfect, unchanging law?

2) If the story preaches a type of law does it also present the message of the Gospel?

3) Are the people real, or are they distorted, and unbelievably good? Your children are sinners in need of God's grace. If the persons in the story do not seem to be in need of forgiveness, your children will receive no direction from the story.

As teachers who believe the message of the Gospel, we have a need and a desire to communicate this fact to our pupils and others about us. There is no one way in which we can express our belief in the Gospel: we do this in many ways, verbal and non-verbal alike. We can express our faith in casual conversation on the street or in the home. In class our belief in Jesus will be reflected in the kinds of comments we make on events, on absences or special achievements of pupils, or on current news. There are times when "being there" is significant. Some of the great moments of life might be in this category: baptisms, confirmations, weddings, funerals.

We are teachers all the time, not only in the church school classroom. Wherever we are, there we are teaching something. In every one of these situations what counts is not *how much* but *what* is said. Let it be plain that our faith is in Christ, not in goodness, or in progress, or in faith itself.

"The Holy Spirit calls me through the Gospel." Let us not neglect to tell this story of salvation freely given in Christ; let us not distort it by changing it into a new law; but let us proclaim it loudly and clearly "that all men may come to the knowledge of Christ."

Suggestions for Discussion:

1. Jot down two of your favorite illustrations, which you have undoubtedly used many times in church school classes. Analyze them. Are they mainly Law, or Gospel? Do they do

what you want them to do? Be ready to share and discuss these illustrations as you have analyzed them.

2. How does the Gospel sometimes get changed into a law?

3. Discuss these statements. Which are Gospel? Which are Law?

    a. You must be born again.

    b. When God forgives He will never accuse you with that particular act of sin again.

    c. If with all your heart you truly seek God, you will surely find Him.

    d. Christians are people who live as God wants them to.

    e. Christians are people whom God has forgiven and made His own.

    f. If you really love the Lord you'll go where He wants you to go.

A Case to Consider: John 3, Nicodemus

Chapter Six

Saved by Grace

That we are saved by grace and not by anything we have deserved is so impressed on the minds of our Lutheran people from childhood that even the least enlightened know it. Yet experience shows us that even the most enlightened persons simply do not understand what it means to be saved by grace, so long as they still are natural men.

This is confirmed again and again whenever a person is awakened to anxiety for the salvation of his soul and begins to think of turning to God. In spite of the fact—which he knows very well and thinks he believes—that if he is to be saved he must be saved by grace, still there is nothing which gives God the Holy Spirit so much trouble as to induce a man to let himself be saved by grace. A man thinks he wants to be saved by grace, but he strives as hard as he can to be saved by something he himself brings about. For this reason he resists and withstands the Spirit's work in his heart, and so hinders his own conversion.

When there is talk of resisting the Holy Spirit most people think of a person who refuses to listen to God's gracious call but continues in his ungodly life. To be sure this is resisting the Holy Spirit. And there are altogether too many who do this. But there are also many who have been spiritually awakened who continue to resist the Holy Spirit by resisting the Gospel's free offer, not permitting God to accept them into His grace as ungodly. They think that it belongs to the regular course of grace that before they can be accepted by God they must become inwardly changed.

God Doesn't Help Us Save Ourselves

They believe, as mentioned, that they cannot save themselves, that they cannot convert themselves, that they cannot remake themselves, that they cannot do anything to deserve salvation, but that everything must come from God and that consequently they must be saved by grace. Therefore they continually pray and implore God to *help* them, and they hope and wait for Him to *help* them. They hope that God will help them to become truly penitent, prepared, "worthy to receive faith," "worthy of grace." And this, to be so *helped* by God, is, they think, to be saved by grace.

In this way one can, to a certain extent at any rate, save his own honor, because he himself can have a hand in it. After all, it is he himself who has brought about his own conversion and salvation, although of course "with God's help." But if everything takes its true course he cannot save his own honor, for all have sinned to the degree that they have fallen short of the glory of God. And he will never be saved in the only way that God saves people until his own conversion, which he is trying to bring about "with God's help," goes so entirely to pieces that his mouth is stopped and he becomes bankrupt.

Christ says, "Apart from me you can do nothing" (John 15:5). Yes, say some, this is just what we think, and therefore we must have His help, for "did we in our own strength confide our striving would be losing."

But the whole context shows that when Jesus says "Apart from me you can do nothing," He does not mean "Without my help you can do nothing." He means, "Except you abide in the fellowship of My life you can do nothing." "As the branch cannot bear fruit by itself, *unless it abides in the vine,* neither can you unless you abide in me." To be able to do anything we must be in the same relation to Jesus as the branch that bears fruit is to the vine, that is, in a living, organic connection.

There are only two conceivable ways by which a man can be saved, by the Law, or by the Gospel. We have seen that by the Law nothing good and acceptable unto God can be produced in an unregenerate person. This is not because the Law is not good, but because the nature of man is so corrupt that far from becoming better through the demands of the Law, it on the contrary takes advantage of the Law to become worse. The Law is therefore weakened by the flesh, as Paul teaches in the eighth chapter of Romans.

But cannot God help an awakened sinner by the Gospel? Yes, He can if the sinner will permit God to rule and will let the help come in the only way in which the Gospel helps sinners. But God's help by means of the Gospel does not consist in the Gospel gradually improving an unregenerate person so that he becomes more and more pleasing in the sight of God and at last is so acceptable that He can grant him faith and accept him as His child.

The Gospel Helps in a Different Way

The Gospel brings help in quite a different way. As already stated, the Gospel is simply an account telling us that Jesus Christ has fulfilled God's Law in our place; that He has atoned, suffered, and paid for all our sins, that the righteousness of God is satisfied, and that God in Christ has reconciled the world unto Himself. The Gospel tells us that we are redeemed by what Jesus has done, and that what Jesus has done is enough for all sinners. Absolutely nothing more is needed. And the Gospel invites all men to come and receive this salvation, saying that we shall get it entirely free, without money and without price, without worthiness and without merit. He that is thirsty, let him but come, and he that will may take the water of life freely.

Or to express it in a different way: The Gospel invites us to believe the message which it brings of salvation through Christ, and it assures us that whoever believes shall be justified—he shall receive the forgiveness of sins—he shall be saved. The Gospel is striving to create this faith, and without man's help the Gospel will create faith in all those who do not stubbornly oppose it. This is grace; this is to be saved by grace; this is to be saved by God.

The first thing, therefore, which must be cultivated and created in a person who is to be saved by grace is faith. As already stated, the Gospel does not gradually make an unregenerate person better and better until at last it brings forth faith in his heart. Before faith comes there is nothing which the Gospel can take hold of and begin to improve; for the old Adam cannot be improved. The only thing which must be done to him is to slay him and drown him after faith has taken up its abode in the heart.

From this we can see what a useless piece of work it is to try to induce God to help us to become fit for grace or prepared to receive faith. The only way in which anything pleasing and acceptable in God's sight can get into a person's heart is by God Himself creating something entirely new there. And what God is always striving to create, and which He by the Gospel's inherent power always does create where the work of His Spirit is not resisted, this is faith. The person in whom God is permitted to create faith is saved by grace.

If you, too, desire to be saved by grace, then believe the Gospel when you hear it. Everything you are trying to do to become more prepared to begin believing, whether you intend to bring about this preparedness by your own power or by God's help, is resistance to grace and the Gospel and makes your conversion and salvation impossible.

Therefore, stop this striving and believe the Gospel. Look away from yourself and look to the Lamb of God who bears the sins of the world. You will never be comforted so long as your eye is turned inward upon yourself, for you will find nothing there which can comfort you. And you will never become better so long as you strive to improve your heart. It cannot be improved. The only way to find comfort is by looking to Jesus. The only way to find salvation is for you as a lost sinner to believe the gospel message of the atonement of Jesus. Therefore, move out of yourself, and move into Christ.

THOUGHTS OF A CHURCH SCHOOL TEACHER

We have seen in this chapter that there is nothing an individual can do to merit God's acceptance of him. All that he can do is believe. All the individual can do is to accept what God has already done. We are saved by grace.

It is God's will that all men be saved and come to the knowledge of truth. When we pray "Thy kingdom come, Thy will be done," we are in a sense pledging ourselves to work toward this end. We become involved in the work of the Holy Spirit.

What is the teacher's role in teaching salvation by grace? Since learning salvation by grace is essentially learning what God has done and said and promised, is not the teacher's role principally that of a witness? The teacher can tell, by words surely, but also by attitudes and actions, what he has seen, learned, and experienced of the saving grace of God. The Holy Spirit makes use of the proclaimer in communicating the good news of the saving grace of God.

Basically the teacher simply tells the story of what God has said and done. Because God's Word and God's acts have to do with people, the teacher also gives evidence of what this Word and these acts mean to him. And this the teacher does whether he is consciously aware of such a testimony or not.

Our pupils not only hear the story of God's love for them: they experience it also, in part, through us. Luther tells us that Christians become "little Christs" to one another. Does it not behoove the teacher, therefore, to become aware of the evidence he gives of what God's saving love means to him?

There are some persons in your class who are easy to love. They are the ones who are pretty or bright or responsive or mannerly. Others are not. However, we are reminded that Christ did not wait for us to become good, or beautiful, or righteous before He demonstrated His love for us. "It was while we were yet sinners that Christ died for us." This knowledge and this experience frees us to help others. "We love, because He first loved us."

The church is called to be a community of the redeemed,

not only in the message it proclaims but also in its fellowship. The classroom can make the communion of saints a reality when teacher and students love one another as Christ has loved them. This excludes no one. God has not commanded these things and then left us to our own devices in trying to fulfill them. The Holy Spirit is with us, working "love, joy, peace, patience, kindness, goodness, faithfulness, gentleness, self-control."

One of the basic steps in trying to show love to an individual—and this may be particularly true of a person who is not very lovable by nature—is an attempt to understand him. When we try to understand, we no longer become merely irritated, we no longer take his actions as personal affront, but rather we grow more sensitive to his needs and more desirous of helping him. We begin to see reasons for his doing things the way he does. We discover that we can give him more constructive ways of dealing with situations, and more constructive outlets for some of his feelings. We can perhaps help him to find a way to satisfy some of his strong emotional needs as well as ways in which he can make positive contributions to the group.

This understanding and concern may not seem to be very directly related to what you are trying to do as a church school teacher. If your only aim is to teach some facts it may not be. If, however, you realize that you are teaching persons with immortal souls—children of God—you will see that there is a connection.

Our words of testimony to what God has said and done can be a meaningless babble if our student is completely wrapped up in his own personal needs and problems. Our words become a mockery if our lives fail to express love and concern and forgiveness. Our words will lack direction and focus if we don't know and understand the person to whom we speak. Our most personal and meaningful words will never be spoken if we don't act to break down the barriers that exist between man and man.

The example of Jesus is certainly a relevant one here. The pages of the Gospel show Him expressing loving forgiveness and acceptance to many individuals with whom we would not want to be seen were they living today. Zacchaeus, for example, was scorned by his fellow townsmen, but was accepted by Jesus. Surely that acceptance was not unrelated to the fact that Jesus was soon able to say to him, "Today salvation is come to this house."

Suggestions for Discussion:

1. Ask yourself, "Who has helped me to know Jesus?" (Not just to know about Him, but to know Him.) Then ask, "How did they do that?" Share your answers with one another. These answers may provide some clues to ways in which the testimony to God's grace can become effective.

2. Can you identify times when you have become aware that your very words or actions in teaching have gotten in the way of the message?

3. How many teachers mislead pupils into thinking that salvation is at least somehow a matter of our deserving it?

A Case to Consider: John 5, The Man at Bethzatha

Chapter Seven

Pointed to Christ

If we are to be saved, it is not enough to know that Christ has done a work *for* us; the Holy Spirit must also be permitted to do a work *in* us. How often has not this truth been heard from our Lutheran pulpits! So our people know this by heart, and it is well that they do. One may have lived for years without having been specially concerned about either the work of Christ or the work of the Holy Spirit. But if one is aroused to serious reflection, it is well to know how necessary it is that the Holy Spirit be permitted to do His work in the heart.

The sinner knows therefore that it is very necessary to permit the Holy Spirit to do a work in us. But he often has only an indistinct and hazy conception of just what the Holy Spirit is to accomplish in his heart. He knows that He will produce something which is good, something from God; but just what this is—well, he really does not know. That is why he does not understand the work of the Holy Spirit in his heart, nor His office, and so hinders His gracious operations.

Since it is the Spirit of God who does this work in the sinner's heart, this work must be something good, something spiritual, something holy, something godly.

The sinner who has been awakened to serious reflection knows that he is evil, carnal, unholy, and ungodly. He longs to feel that he is becoming different in this respect. To be permitted to know, feel, and be conscious of the work of the Spirit, which means in his opinion to be permitted to feel that he is becoming spiritual, holy, and godly, would be very delightful.

So he goes about waiting to see, as it were, the work of the Holy Spirit. He wants to know and feel how the Holy Spirit removes whatever is wicked, carnal, and unholy from the heart, and replaces it with something good, spiritual, holy, godly, and therefore acceptable unto God, so that he himself can, so to speak, keep pace with the change and improvement.

However, as time goes on he doesn't feel that any such improvement is taking place in him. On the contrary, as before indicated, he only feels worse and more ungodly and thinks that his case is more and more hopeless. And when he experiences no such improvement within himself, he concludes that the Holy Spirit is not working in him at all. Yet the Spirit is all this time continuing His blessed work. But because the sinner does not understand the work of the Holy Spirit, he misunderstands what He already has accomplished in him as well as what He is still striving to bring about in his heart.

The Holy Spirit's Work in Conversion

What then is the Holy Spirit's work in conversion? To begin with, His work is to make the sinner feel and know that he is ungodly, sinful, and corrupt. It is a result of the work of the Holy Spirit that the sinner has begun to think seriously about his relation to God, that he is anxious about his soul's salvation, that he is dissatisfied with his condition, that he is without peace and without comfort, that his own attempts to improve have proved such an utter failure, that he is perplexed and embarrassed about it, and that in spite of all he has tried he sees himself hopelessly lost. All this the Holy Spirit has accomplished in his heart.

It is the Holy Spirit who has awakened him to serious meditation and reflection. It is the Holy Spirit who shows him how utterly ungodly, wicked, and thoroughly corrupt he is. It is the Holy Spirit who persists in convincing him how utterly powerless and incapable he is to correct the wickedness which is in his heart. It is the Holy Spirit who continues to teach him that the corruption in him is so great and so complete that he cannot be improved or gradually become godlier, more spiritual, and more pleasing unto God. All this is the Spirit's work. It is self-evident that this work is not of such a nature that he who is the object of it can feel that anything good and godly is about to come forth in his soul.

Why does the Holy Spirit strive to make him so miserable, so dejected, and so forlorn? Because those who are well have no need of a physician, but those who are sick. And the Holy Spirit desires earnestly that the poor sinner should come to the Physician, to the only One who can help and save him, namely, to the Lord Jesus Christ. When, therefore, the Holy Spirit makes the sinner so despondent and dejected, yes, utterly lost, it is because it is only a needed preparatory work for His proper work in conversion, namely to declare Christ to the sinner.

No do-it-yourself kit.

The Important Thing Is to See Christ

We have said that many spiritually awakened souls are striving to see and feel the work of the Holy Spirit in their hearts. However, they are not saved by seeing the Holy Spirit, but by seeing Christ. To enable a sinner to see Christ is the Holy Spirit's work. It is therefore not important for the Spirit to present or show Himself. No, there is another whom He wants to present and bring forward, and that is Christ.

Before Christ left this world with His visible presence He said to His disciples that He, after His departure, would send them the Holy Spirit, the Spirit of truth. When He should come, said Jesus, "He will glorify me, for He will take what is mine and declare it to you."

Jesus has taught us that this is eternal life, that we know the only true God and Him whom He has sent, namely, Jesus Christ. "And there is salvation in no one else, for there is no other name under heaven given among men" whereby anyone can be saved, except the name of Jesus Christ. In Jesus the sinner must find his whole salvation; in Him he must find all that he lacks. In Jesus he must find all that he in vain has sought to find in his own heart and has tried "by God's help" to bring about in himself. In Jesus he must find all that he had thought the Holy Spirit should bring forth in his own soul.

To show him, to get him to understand, and to persuade him to believe that all this is in Christ is the Holy Spirit's work. It is His work to persuade the sinner to look away from himself and his attempts at improvement, and to look to Jesus only. It is the Holy Spirit's work to create the belief in the heart of the sinner that he is acceptable to God solely because Christ has redeemed him. It is the work of the Spirit to produce in the heart of a sinner a confidence that God will accept him, make him His child, and forgive him all his sins solely because Jesus has died for him. It is the work of the Holy Spirit to persuade the sinner to believe that he is saved by grace only. When the sinner believes this, the work of the Holy Spirit is being accomplished in him.

It may be that he is not conscious that the Spirit is doing His work in him. The Holy Spirit does His work regardless of whether man knows it is His work which is now being done or whether He receives any credit for it—if only Christ receives thanks for His work.

But does not the Holy Spirit effect such a change in the heart of a sinner that he is conscious of having become a new creature, that the old things have passed away and all things have become new? Does not a noticeable change take place as a result of the work of the Holy Spirit so that a person really becomes more godly, spiritual, and holy?—so that a person knows that he loves God and everything godly and so that he really begins to hate sin and get power over it?

Yes, that is certainly true. "If any one is in Christ, he is a new creation" (II Cor. 5:17). What does this Word of God say? It says, *"If any one is in Christ,"* then he is a new creation. It does not say that the Holy Spirit is gradually making him a new creature until He finally gets him so renewed that He can bring Him into Christ. No, he must come into Christ as an ungodly creature. He must begin by believing in Christ, and *then* he becomes a new creature. No matter how difficult this often seems to be for troubled souls, it is nevertheless the *only* way to life.

"To him who does not work, but trusts Him who justifies *the ungodly,* his faith is reckoned as righteousness" (Rom. 4:5). In the thirty-first chapter of Jeremiah the Lord explains how such a change takes place in the hearts of people who find delight in the Law of God and get a willingness to do His will. He says in verse 33, "I will put my Law within them, and I will write it upon their hearts." Then in the next verse He says, "*For* I will forgive their iniquity, and I will remember their sin no more."

The fact that their sins have been forgiven explains why such a change has taken place in their hearts. Jesus also taught this when the sinful woman stood at His feet and wept. He said, "*Her sins, which are many, are forgiven;* for she loved much." First believe; believe as one who is unworthy—as one who is ungodly —then the change will come as a fruit of that.

THOUGHTS OF A CHURCH SCHOOL TEACHER

As teachers we earnestly desire and pray that we shall be successful in our work with the members of our class. Yet, it doesn't always happen this way. There are times when our prayers seem to go unanswered and our labors seem to bear no fruit. We can easily grow discouraged.

That Jesus was conscious of the problems involved in "sowing" the word is shown in His parable of the sower. Conditions differ. Individuals differ. Even the ministry of Jesus was not completely successful according to most current evaluation standards. During Jesus' lifetime the disciples never fully understood who He was or why He was here. Among the twelve, Peter denied Him and Judas betrayed

Him. It doesn't sound like a very promising beginning, yet it changed the course of all of history.

As teachers, we want so badly to *see* results—but faith and the stages that may precede it are not very clearly "see-able." We may therefore be tempted to press for results that we *can* see.

- Sometimes we look for satisfaction in the quantity of catechism or number of Bible verses that can be recited by the individual.
- Sometimes we look for pious platitudes or "right" phrases in response to a question or situation, without looking behind these for any depth of meaning or experience, or being able to interpret what we see when we do look.
- Sometimes we press for more sanctified lives among our students and obtain mere legalistic conformity.

There are dangers in wanting to *see* too many results, for these results may well be the result of the workings of the teacher and not the results of the working of the Holy Spirit. Sometimes as teachers we are very conscious of the great necessity of seeing our sinfulness to the point of needing very desperately to find a Savior. We may be sucked into the terrible role of playing God, of preaching specific sins, binding "burdens heavy to be borne," and manipulating the person into terrified acknowledgement of his depravity.

This usurping of the work of the Holy Spirit is a dreadful temptation to many, especially the most pious, who want to *produce* in others the travail of soul that has meant much to them. But only the Spirit knows what each one needs!

The role of the teacher is to present the Law as it is, not with new additions. And to present the story of Christ as it is, not with new exhortations of law. The ultimate work is that of the Spirit for whose presence and guidance the teacher will constantly and expectantly pray.

Mature Christian faith does not come about quickly or easily. In other areas of life we are content to have persons learn and develop at their own rate. We expect to find a marked difference between the reading ability of the first grader and the fifth grader. We are not surprised that the

16-year-old boy is stronger than his ten-year-old brother. Yet, sometimes we are disappointed when in six months or a year our students fail to reach our own level of spiritual maturity. Remember this has taken many years, many experiences, and learning from many formal and informal Christian teachers.

As we ourselves are pointed to Christ the Spirit works within us. And one of His fruits is faithfulness—not necessarily successfulness, but faithfulness. As this faithfulness to our calling as teachers grows, we realize more truly our place, and are willing to say with Paul, "I planted, Apollos watered, but God gave the growth."

Suggestions for Discussion:

1. It has sometimes been said that much of what happens in a Sunday school class is character training but not Christian education. Can you see the difference? Which is happening in your church school class?

2. What results of Christian teaching have you seen in your class?

3. What expectation do your pupils have for one another as Christians?

A Case to Consider: 2 Kings 5, Naaman

Chapter Eight

Faith

As far back as we can remember that we have had any knowledge of Christianity we have known that we are justified and saved by faith. This we have, so to speak, imbibed with the mother's milk. It has been told us in almost every sermon we have heard. So if there is anything we Lutherans ought to know, it is this. And if these things could be learned by using our natural faculties, then we should all have learned and understood them. But it is apparent here, too, that the natural man does not receive the things of the Spirit of God. One can, it is true, learn to use the right words to express sound doctrine; but to learn to understand what the words really mean, this one cannot do before God has performed the miracle of opening his blind eyes so that he can see.

What really is faith? Many people have a very vague and indistinct conception of it; but at any rate they think they know this about faith; that it is a kind of feeling in the heart which causes the fear of God's wrath and punishment to be taken away and makes them feel secure. Just why fear should disappear and why they should feel calm and secure they may not know. But they have learned that it is a gift from God, a grace of God. So they go about longing for this feeling, and when it does not come they feel insecure and fearful. This erroneous belief, that faith is a feeling, has caused much harm.

Now it is no doubt true that where there is faith there is also a variety of feelings. Christianity is not a religion devoid of feeling. In this Christianity rises above all other religions, for it is the only religion which gives peace to the heart of man and makes him happy and blessed. In the heart of a believer there are feelings of both sin and grace, of both doubt and trust, of both fear and hope, of both sorrow and joy.

Faith Is Not the Same as Feeling

But faith is not the same as feeling. The Scriptures say that faith is "the conviction of things not seen" (Heb. 11:1). It is a conviction of something which cannot be grasped by any of the human senses. Faith can no more feel the things it is convinced of than it can see them. It is indeed true that faith is something in the heart which makes the fear of God's wrath and punishment disappear and makes one feel secure. Faith is convinced of God's grace and friendship, and such a conviction is incompatible with fear of God's wrath and punishment. Therefore we read in the Epistle to the Romans that since we are justified by faith we have peace with God. But this sense of security and peace is not founded on any elusive feeling which one may have in the heart. It is founded upon a conviction of truth, a fact about which God has given information and enlightenment.

What is this truth, this fact of which faith is a conviction? It is a truth and a fact which the Word of

God tells us. Faith does not rest, therefore, on something which I find in my own heart. Faith is not directed to something which exists within myself. Faith rests on the Word of God. Faith is directed to something which the Gospel holds forth. Faith is directed not inwardly, but outwardly. Faith is the Holy Spirit's work in the heart. However, this work of the Holy Spirit which is going on in the heart is not concerned with the heart itself, but with something outside it—not with something which is now taking place inside one's own soul, but with something which took place nineteen hundred years ago. Because of this, faith can be a firm conviction rather than an uncertain supposition or a hope that something may possibly be true.

The Content of Faith

What is it that faith believes? It believes the testimony which God has given about His Son; it believes the Gospel; it believes in Jesus, who has redeemed us. It believes that He has fulfilled God's Law in our place, that He has suffered for all our sins, and that He has in this way acquired for us God's grace, the forgiveness of sins, sonship, life, and eternal salvation.

Yes, but Jesus has done this for all men, has He not? Of course He has. Isn't it just that which is so grand and joyful? Isn't it just because of this fact that I can be sure that He has also redeemed me, atoned for my sins, and obtained forgiveness of sins, sonship, life, and salvation for me?

But must I not believe something special about myself? Isn't it true that in spite of the fact that Christ has redeemed all men, not all are under grace? It is necessary, is it not, that I personally come into such a state that I no longer am under wrath and condemnation? In this way many a poor, blinded sinner continues to struggle against grace and to bring objections against the Gospel and the beloved Savior who in the Gospel stands with outstretched arms of grace to receive him!

No, you are not at all to believe anything special about yourself! You are not so important or select a person that it is necessary to do something extra to save you. You are only an ordinary sinner like all the others of whom it is said that "all have sinned and fall short of the glory of God"; and that they are "justified by His grace as a gift through the redemption which is in Christ Jesus" (Rom. 3:23, 24). You are included in this "all" both in respect to sin and in respect to salvation.

This is the great fault of so many, that they will not place themselves in the same class with all other sinners and will not believe that what God has found to be enough for the whole world is also enough for them. God once said to Paul, "My grace is sufficient for you." If God believes that it is enough, and if it was enough for Paul, should it not then be enough for you, too? It is, to be sure, true that although Christ has redeemed all men, still not all are under grace. But why are they outside of grace? Because they do not believe in the grace which is for all.

Sin Shuts People Out From God

What is it that shuts people out from God and salvation? It is sin in all its extent and in all its forms—that one does not love, fear, and trust in God. It is that the heart is constantly inclined to evil, that there are evil lusts and desires in the heart.

Now, what has Christ done to save us from all this sin? He became the Lamb of God who takes away the sin of the world, and therefore also your sin. He bore our sins in His body on the tree. He was wounded for our transgressions. He was bruised for our iniquities. He suffered the punishment that all had deserved. He atoned for sin and thus earned forgiveness of sins for all, also for you.

Isn't that enough? What more could be done for you? It is what Christ has done for all that faith believes—nothing else. This faith clings to, depends on, rests on, builds on, places its trust in, and finds its only comfort in. And it is when one believes this that a feeling of security and peace comes into the heart, as a fruit and result of believing the Gospel.

We do not build on our faith, but on Christ. We feel safe and confident, not because we find a faith in our hearts with which we can be satisfied, but because our faith has obtained an insight into the atonement of Christ and finds that God has declared Himself to be satisfied with it. We do not occupy ourselves with our faith, but our faith occupies itself with Christ and finds all that it lacks and all that it needs in Him. Therefore Paul said he did not know anything except Jesus Christ and Him crucified.

So it is with everyone who believes. Everyone who is spiritually awakened and converted as an adult has many and various kinds of experiences, but it is not because of these experiences that he believes himself to be saved. It is not his contrition nor penitence; it is not a conversion experience. It is not that he has become a new creature; it is not his faith, not his prayers —none of these things gives him the courage to believe himself to be a child of God.

Only one thing gives a sinner boldness to enter into the presence of God, and that is the blood of Jesus Christ. Not a little boldness is required for a sinner to believe that God should want to accept him into fellowship with Himself. And so long as he continues to search in his own heart for something to give him this boldness he will not find it. But if he looks at the blood that was shed on the cross for the forgiveness of sins, then the boldness will come.

THOUGHTS OF A CHURCH SCHOOL TEACHER

One of the first things, and certainly the most important thing that the infant learns is trust. Since he is so completely helpless he can do nothing but trust in those about him to satisfy his needs. The circle of those in whom he has faith widens as he grows older. As he awakens to the fact that he is a child of God, adopted by Him in Baptism, his faith in God will become a conscious thing.

What is faith? Perhaps trust is as good a term as any to define it. We sometimes see it in human relationships. The little child may awaken during the thunder storm very much afraid, but will grow calm when enfolded in the arms of mother whose words he believes and whom he trusts to care for him.

However, people have limitations; they are not always dependable. They are not always consistent. In contrast, the hymnwriter expresses his complete trust in God in these words:

> *In heavenly love abiding,*
> *No change my heart shall fear;*
> *And safe is such confiding,*
> *For nothing changes here:*
> *The storm may roar without me,*

My heart may low be laid,
But God is round about me,
And can I be dismayed?

We want our students to grow in faith. As you can see, this is different from sheer knowledge or intellectual belief.

What then is our role as teachers? When our students can recite the names of the books of the Bible we can know that they have learned some information. But, has their faith grown stronger? We may teach them the right words and phrases, "but the Lord looks on the heart."

You have probably heard the expression, "Faith is caught, not taught." There is an element of truth in it. As you think of your own Christian experience, you will probably discover one or more persons from whom you, to some extent, "caught" a vision of what faith is. To some extent the strength of the Sunday school movement has been just this: the evident and contagious faith of those who have dedicated time and energies to teaching. The message of the Gospel somehow becomes more real and relevant as we see it reflected in the life of someone we know and respect and love.

Ultimately, of course, it is the Holy Spirit who leads the individual to faith in Christ as Savior and Lord. We can teach the Word but the Holy Spirit alone can work in the heart of an individual so that he responds to the Word. We can present the Word of God and guide pupils to think through what it means, but the Holy Spirit alone can draw men to Christ.

Suggestions for Discussion:

1. What, in relation to your own faith, have you been *taught*? What have you *caught*? Is there still more to it than is expressed by these terms?

2. What, really, was the purpose of your lesson last Sunday?

3. Think about the "best" student in your class, and about the "poorest" student. What do you think each is really getting from his church school experience?

A Case to Consider: Matthew 8:5-13, The Centurion

Chapter Nine

The Forgiveness of Sins

Sin! What a sum of affliction, sorrow, and misfortune is included in this word! How much unrest, anxiety, and concern sin has caused! There are many, it is true, who are not troubled by sin. But this is because they are sleeping. One is not troubled with anxiety when he is asleep. But all who are awake are more or less anxious and uneasy because of sin.

The wickedness, deep depravity, and evil inclination of our natures cause the greatest anxiety. There may be deep sorrow and anxiety also because of sinful deeds, words, and thoughts when one is awakened and sees them in the holy light of God's Law. But the greatest and most constant source of anxiety is the evil heart, absence of love to God, and lack of fear of God and trust in God, together with a constant inclination to what is evil. "The heart is deceitful above all things, and desperately corrupt; who can understand it?" (Jer. 17:9).

What is to be done with sin? What has been done cannot be undone. The sin which I have committed is committed. If I wish ever so much that what has been done might be undone; if I repent ever so much; if I could weep tears of blood; still what has been done will never be undone. Nor can I remodel my evil and deceitful heart. I cannot escape from myself; I cannot get away from being a sinner. And he who sins shall die; that is the judgment. There is a way out of the difficulty only if God will be gracious unto me and forgive me my sins.

And does not God's Word say that God forgives sin—yes, that He is very generous in forgiving? It says that He will abundantly pardon, that the Lord is a merciful and gracious God, longsuffering and abounding in mercy and truth, and that He forgives iniquity, transgression, and sin. Therefore the prophet Micah exclaims, "Who is a God like Thee, pardoning iniquity and passing over transgression for the remnant of His inheritance? He does not retain His anger forever because He delights in steadfast love. He will again have compassion upon us, He will tread our iniquities under foot. Thou wilt cast all our sins into the depths of the sea." Therefore we find that when any one who was troubled about his sin came to Jesus, he was told, "Be of good cheer, your sins are forgiven."

How Can I Be Sure?

"But," says many a sinner who has been awakened to anxiety over his sin, "how can I be sure of the forgiveness of my sins? I see in God's Word that God forgives sin, yes, is willing to forgive sin; but how can I know that He has forgiven me my sins?"

"I wish," many a person sighs, "that I could have lived at the time of Christ, so that I like Nicodemus could have gone to Jesus and spoken to Him privately!"

"If only I could have been in the place of the man sick of the palsy and have heard Jesus say to me personally, 'Your sins are forgiven.' Yes, then I could be entirely sure of the forgiveness of my sins, for then I would have a word from God Himself on which to build the assurance of forgiveness."

"If only I might look into the Book of God and assure myself that He really has blotted out of it all my sins! Or if I only could hear a voice in my own heart telling me clearly and distinctly that God has forgiven my sins. But Jesus no more visibly walks about on earth so that we can speak to Him; and no human eye is permitted to read what is written in the Book of God. So there doesn't seem to be any way by which one can be sure of the forgiveness of his sins."

"Oh," some may say, "one can feel that his sins are forgiven." Yes, he thinks he can perceive it; he feels it and is glad and happy because the burden of his sins has been taken away—he is free. But before he realizes it, this feeling is gone, and the joy and peace and freedom are also gone, and he begins to doubt that the feeling he had was to be depended on. Is the sin forgiven, or not? God alone knows. So there he is once more in uncertainty. And so long as he lives in this uncertainty, constantly hovering between fear and hope, he will have no strength, no boldness, no peace, and no joy. He tries again to work up this feeling in himself and prays God to give him that sweet sensation again. At times he may feel easier and begin again to hope that everything will be better. But then the feeling again disappears and he sinks back into despondency and dejection because he cannot be sure of the forgiveness of his sins.

Forgiveness Must Be Believed

Let us remember the plain and simple truth which we learned in our Catechism, namely, that the forgiveness of sins is something which must be *believed*. "I *believe* in the forgiveness of sins." Isn't that what we learned to say in the Third Article? We do not feel the forgiveness of sins; neither do we hope that we shall receive forgiveness. But we *believe* the forgiveness of sins.

When we say we believe the forgiveness of sins, we do not mean the same thing as when we say that we believe we shall have fine weather tomorrow. The Christian faith, whereby one believes the forgiveness of sins, is not more or less probable supposition or conjecture. Faith is, as stated in Hebrews, an *assurance* of things hoped for, a *conviction* of things not seen. It is therefore an assurance and conviction of something which exists but which I do not see and which, we may add, I cannot feel.

Let us in the next place notice that what God says we shall believe must be true whether we believe it or not. It is not our faith which makes truth out of whatever we believe. It is a great error, in which many seem to be ensnared, to suppose that what we believe really comes into existence on account of our faith. No, faith creates nothing; faith only believes what God says. Only that is a Christian faith which builds on the Word of God. I can have no faith in something about which God has said nothing. If I am to believe anything with a Christian faith I must have God's Word for it. If, therefore, I am to believe the remission of sins I must have a word from God on which to build this faith, or else my so-called "faith" will be only a loose conjecture or guesswork.

But does Scripture say that *my* sin has been forgiven *me*? No. Well, there I am. Yes, and many stand at just that point and hence constantly live in uncertainty about the forgiveness of their sins—because they have not learned on what to build the certainty of forgiveness.

Forgiveness Is Not Separate from Redemption

The forgiveness of sins must never be separated from the redemption of Christ; it must never be sought as something separate, but must always be sought in Christ. Therefore Jesus says, "This is my blood of the covenant which is poured out for many for the remission of sins." Jesus shed His blood on the cross in order that the remission of sins in this way should be provided.

There are many who seem to think that we must influence the heart of God and induce Him to be willing to forgive our sins. Because it is impossible to find out whether we have done what must be done (prayed fervently enough, believed intensely enough, etc.) for this, it is also impossible to become sure that He has forgiven us our sins. So we continue to live in uncertainty and insecurity.

Something else than prayers and tears and exertion was needed to obtain the remission of sins. "Without the shedding of blood there is no forgiveness of sins." But Christ shed His blood for the remission of sins, and ever since then the remission of sins has been prepared. The remission of sins is something which we find all ready for us in Christ. Therefore Paul says, "In Him we have redemption through His blood, the forgiveness of our trespasses."

The redemption of Christ is the remission of sins, according to what Paul says. Redemption consisted in this, that Christ procured the remission of sins for us. It was from sin and all that goes with it that He redeemed us. This He did not do by taking sin out of the world, nor by doing away with the fact that we are sinners. He did it by procuring the forgiveness of our sins. This is what the redemption of Christ is. Therefore the Scriptures teach that "God was in Christ reconciling the world to Himself, not counting their trespasses against them."

To believe the remission of sins is therefore the same as to believe that Christ has redeemed us. You cannot believe the one without believing the other. Sometimes people say, "I believe that Jesus has redeemed me, but I cannot believe in the forgiveness of sins." Such a saying is a complete self-contradiction. He who does not believe in the forgiveness of sins does not believe that Christ has redeemed him. If he says he believes that Christ has redeemed him but does not believe in the forgiveness of sins, he shows that he simply does not understand what it means to say that Christ redeemed him; he does not know what is meant by the word "redemption." As before stated, redemption consists in this, that the remission of sins has been procured.

Belief Is Built on God's Word

When, therefore I believe the remission of sins, I build this belief on a Word from God. I build on the

testimony which God has given concerning His Son:
I build on the Gospel of the redemption of Christ. I
believe what the Word of God says, namely, that the
blood of Christ was shed for the remission of sins. I
believe that we in His blood have redemption, that is,
the remission of sins.

The remission of sins must therefore be sought and
found in Christ and His redemption. No other forgiveness can be found; there is no other forgiveness to be
had. I must not delve into my own heart to find the
forgiveness of sins; it is not to be found there. I must
not hunt in my heart to try to find something which
will permit me to believe the forgiveness of sins, or
which can give me an assurance of forgiveness. I must
hunt in the Word of God—in the Gospel. There I shall
find a firm foundation.

I can confidently depend on what God has said; and
Christ Himself says in the Gospel that He shed His
blood for the remission of sins. The Word of God says
that Christ gave Himself as a ransom for all, and that
we in His blood have the remission of sins. This is
something worth building on. This is something quite
different from the feelings and moods of the deceitful
heart. This is the firm rock which shall stand when
heaven and earth will have passed away.

But is not this mixing together things that do not
belong together? Is not this mixing the works of Christ
and the works of the Holy Spirit? We read about redemption in the Second Article, but about the remission
of sins in the Third Article. That is true, but still this
is not mixing together things that do not belong together
for there is the closest connection between the Second
and Third Articles.

It is the work of the Holy Spirit when a man *believes* the forgiveness of sins, and therefore it comes in the Third Article. But that there is any remission of sins to believe is the work of Christ and comes therefore in the Second Article. The Second Article is the prerequisite to the Third Article. The Holy Spirit could create no faith in us unless the Lord Jesus Christ had procured that which faith grasps.

Therefore Jesus said to His disciples that it was expedient for them that He should go away, for if He did not go away the Comforter would not come. But if He went away He would send the Spirit who should bear witness of Christ and declare Christ unto them. This the Holy Spirit does every time a man believes in the forgiveness of sins; for no one has any other forgiveness to believe in than what Christ procured when He went away.

But, you may object, when Jesus through suffering and death went away, He acquired the remission of sins for all people, did He not? And one must after all distinguish between the redemption of Jesus for all and the individual's participation in this salvation. The remission of sins is after all something personal which concerns me, and me only. Isn't it true, that although Christ has acquired the remission of sins for all, there are still many persons whose sins are not forgiven? Isn't it true that if I am to have my sins forgiven, God must deal with *me*? God must absolve me and forgive my sins, or else the redemption of Christ is of no benefit to me. And how can I be sure that God really has absolved me and forgiven me? How can I be sure that the remission which Christ procured for all men has become my personal possession so that I have become a partaker of it? This question many troubled and sincere seekers cannot answer.

It is true that the acquiring is one thing and participation another. It is true there are many persons whose sins are not forgiven although Christ has acquired remission for all. But we must not let Satan use this truth to obscure another truth so that we see nothing clearly.

Let us turn to Acts 10:43. There we read, "To Him [Christ] all the prophets bear witness that every one who believes in Him receives forgiveness of sins through His name." This passage speaks of *receiving* the forgiveness of sins so that one really possesses it. Consequently it speaks of really being absolved, of really having one's sins forgiven. And Peter says in this passage that it is the unanimous testimony of all the prophets that everyone who believes in Him receives the remission of sins.

Everyone Who Believes Is Forgiven

Do you believe in Jesus? Do you believe He is the Messiah, the Son of God? Do you believe that He died and rose again? Do you believe He is the Lamb of God who takes away the sin of the world? Do you believe He has atoned for the sin of the world? Do you believe we in His blood have redemption, the remission of sins? Do you believe that He shed His blood for the remission of sins?

You do believe that, do you not? You do not believe God is a liar when He in the Gospel has testified all this about His Son? You do believe, even though you like the father of the epileptic boy must cry out, "I believe; help my unbelief." But if you believe this, then according to this passage you have the forgiveness of your sins; for does it not say that *every one* who believes in Him *receives* the forgiveness of sins?

There you have a Word from God to prove that your sins have been forgiven. And how do you receive the forgiveness of your sins, according to this Bible passage? By believing in Christ. Every one who believes in Him receives the remission of sins. Paul teaches the same in a sermon which he delivered in Antioch in Pisidia, which we read in the thirteenth chapter of Acts. There he says, "Let it be known to you therefore, brethren, that through this man forgiveness of sins is proclaimed to you, and by Him every one that believes is freed from everything from which you could not be freed by the Law of Moses." Thus we see that the remission of sins is proclaimed in the Gospel, and that everyone who believes is justified. "God acquits him of sin and its punishment and regards him in Christ as if he never had sinned."

But how can it be that faith in Christ has such an effect that sin thereby is forgiven us? It is this way: God has given us His Son. In Him we find all that belongs to our salvation. Our redemption, entire and complete, is in Christ. He who now believes in Christ receives Christ, accepts Him, and is made partaker of Christ and all that He is and has, including the remission of sins. The remission of sins is not received as something which is given separately. The remission of sins must, as previously stated, never be separated from Christ and must never be sought except in connection with Christ. He therefore who believes in Christ or—which is the same thing—by faith accepts Christ, he receives therewith the remission of sins.

When people in the Old Covenant ate the Passover Lamb they had to eat the *whole* lamb. They could not choose a part of it and leave a part (Ex. 12:10). So it is with Christ, of whom the Passover Lamb was a type. One cannot accept a part of Christ and not another part. One cannot by faith accept and possess a part of what Christ has procured for us and not accept and possess the other part. One cannot accept redemption and not the remission of sins. If you believe in Christ you receive the whole Christ so that there is absolutely nothing which belongs to your pardon, sonship, salvation, or eternal happiness which you then do not receive. Therefore Paul says in Romans 8:32, "He who did not spare His own Son but gave him up for us all, will He not also give us all things with Him?" And therefore the same apostle says in 1 Corinthians 3:21, "For all things are yours." And therefore we read in one of our beautiful hymns:

> *We have all things, Christ possessing;*
> *Life eternal, second birth;*
> *Present pardon, peace and blessing,*
> *While we tarry here on earth.*

We repeat it: so long as we persist in hunting in our own hearts for some kind of feeling or something else, whatever name it may have, on which we can build the assurance of the remission of our sins, just so long do we fail to get assurance. So long as we wait for something to come into our hearts to convince us that now our sins are forgiven, just so long we shall wait in vain. But if we turn our eye away from ourselves and toward Christ, and believe the Word of God which says that Christ redeemed us and that we in His blood have redemption, the remission of sins, then we have a firm foundation to stand on.

Isn't it enough that Christ has redeemed us? Isn't it enough that Christ has earned the remission of sins for us? We surely don't want any other remission than that which Christ has acquired for us, do we? Surely it has cost our Savior dearly enough to procure the forgiveness of sins for us. We ought to honor Him for what He has done. And then we ought truly to thank Him and not wound Him with unbelief by searching elsewhere to find the remission of sins and peace for our hearts. Remember, we have all in Christ, and that is enough.

> *And when you find Him,*
> *Then you have found all*
> *That ever your heart can desire.*

THOUGHTS OF A CHURCH SCHOOL TEACHER

I believe in "the forgiveness of sins." How many times have you said these words? They are a part of our confession of faith in the words of the Apostles' Creed. As a teacher, I believe in the forgiveness of sins.

I believe that God forgives me when I am so busy teaching the lesson that I forget about the children, or grow impatient with them.

I believe that God forgives me when I twist the Gospel into new law.

I believe that God forgives me when I am so busy talking myself that I do not have time to listen to the children.

I believe that God forgives me when I give my students the idea that if they try hard enough to be good they can please God.

I believe that God forgives me when I am too concerned with other things to spend time preparing to teach His children.

I believe that God forgives me when I forget to use or leave undeveloped the talents and potentialities that He has created within His children.

With forgiveness comes release. The burden has been lifted. The weights that would drag behind us and would bring us to a slow, grinding halt have been removed. We can start over again. We can begin with fresh resolve and new enthusiasm.

Our students declare these words with us, "I believe in the forgiveness of sins." How much of a reality is this to them? Can you help them to see that this belief is based not on their feelings but on the Word of God which tells us that through Christ we have the forgiveness of sins?

There is also a horizontal aspect to this question of forgiveness. We express this in the Lord's Prayer when we say, "Forgive us our trespasses as we forgive those who trespass against us." Just as forgiveness is necessary to restore us to fellowship with God, so forgiveness is necessary in our relationships with our fellow men. We cannot deal effectively with each other so long as we have not forgiven one another. Do you remember how the disciples asked Jesus how often they should forgive their brother? Jesus told them, "I do not say to you seven times, but 70 times seven."

Just as daily renewal is a part of our relationship with God, so, too, there is a type of renewal that takes place in our personal relationships as we forgive and are forgiven. Even as our Christian experience and faith become strengthened when we accept the forgiveness offered to us in Christ, so the renewal of personal relationships involves new discovery of self and of the other person, and a consequent strengthening of the relationship.

Certainly forgiveness is of critical importance in our relationship with our students.

Part of our role as teachers is to show and express forgiveness to our students. As long as we allow hostility or antagonism to remain between us we are less effective instruments for God in our work in His Kingdom.

Suggestions for Discussion:

1. Ask your pupils to tell what they think forgiveness is. Then ask them how they can be forgiven by God. Their answers will show you some of their central concepts of how forgiveness may take place in their own lives.

2. Are you forgiven?

3. When your pupils observe you from week to week are they helped or hindered in gaining an understanding of forgiveness?

A Case to Consider:
Acts 8:26-39, The Ethiopian Eunuch

Faith and Feeling

We have said that Christianity is not a religion destitute of feeling. On the contrary, no religion produces so many and such intense feelings in the heart as Christianity. Now it is true that not all persons are equally emotional, and not all persons show their feelings to the same degree. But surely it may safely be said that there is not a single adult who has been converted and has come into fellowship with God by faith in Jesus who, when he has received grace to believe himself saved for the sake of Jesus Christ alone, does not experience a great joy and peace in his heart.

Especially is this true if he has been laboring under the Law for some time, has felt himself lost and condemned to eternal death, has striven and struggled to become better, and then only found that he was becoming worse and worse so that he was almost driven to despair. When finally his eyes are opened to the fact that he is saved by the redemption which is in Christ Jesus, is it strange that such a person becomes overjoyed? Is it strange that when the Lord "restores the fortunes of Zion," that one becomes like those who dream, that one's mouth is filled with laughter and one's tongue with shouts of joy, as we read in Psalm 126?

He who thinks that it is strange has no understanding of what it means to get out of the darkness into God's marvelous light, to be delivered from the bondage of sin and the Law and be ushered into the glorious liberty of grace and the Gospel. Is it strange if he who has been in the greatest anxiety which can be found in the heart of man—unrest and anguish at being condemned —experiences a peace which passes all understanding when he sees and knows that he is saved? If Romans 5:1 is true, namely that since we are justified by faith we have peace with God through our Lord Jesus Christ, then peace must come into the heart that believes in Jesus. Such a soul not only knows that peace is made by Christ, but he feels, experiences, and enjoys that peace.

> *Oh, how my spirit doth rejoice,*
> *Since I my Jesus found.*

Feelings Don't Last

But it is a common experience of men that no emotion, whether it be a feeling of pain and sorrow or of joy and delight, can endure with the same strength for any length of time. In this respect religious feelings are not essentially different from other feelings. Another experience common to men is that we are most overcome by emotions when we experience something new. When this new experience is no longer new, but becomes commonplace, then the strong emotions vanish. When two young people fall in love and become engaged, this love to begin with is attended by very intense feelings. But when they have been married for some time, this feeling passes away. This certainly does not mean that they no longer love each other as much as before; but love expresses itself in another and usually more sensible way.

This is also the experience that many newly-converted persons have, and it is an experience which has caused much anxiety and many conflicts of soul. The person who after many conflicts finds rest in the gracious bosom of Jesus thinks perhaps as Peter did that it is good to be there and desires to build and live there forever. Inexperienced as he is in regard to the conditions of the Christian life, he may think that if it is so blessed to be a child of God in the very beginning, what will it not be when he has made some progress, has grown in grace, and has had richer experiences!

Then perhaps he notices that the delightful and blessed feelings, far from increasing in strength, on the contrary begin to pass away; that joy decreases, and that peace no longer is undisturbed. He notices also that the sin in his heart is not so completely dead and gone, but on the contrary, evil desires, sinful thoughts— in short the nature of the old Adam—again make their presence known. He may have thought that when the old things had passed away and all had become new he would also get rid of the feeling of evil in his own heart. And in the first great joy and sensation of the new life which he experienced, he felt very little of the nature of the old man. The little he did feel he thought he would entirely overcome as he gradually became stronger in his life with God. Instead he perceives that so much, so deplorably much, of the old man remains.

Under such circumstances, many a newly-converted soul has become alarmed and terrified. As the blessed feelings disappear, he believes that he is losing life itself. As the feelings of grace disappear, he thinks it is grace that he is losing. Or perhaps he begins to doubt that he really did experience God's saving and converting grace. Maybe it was nothing but a delusion.

Now let us reflect a little. When you obtained peace, what was it that brought it? Was it that you felt that the condition of your heart had become as you thought it ought to be? No, it was because now you could look away from yourself and your own heart and could look to Jesus, letting your eye remain on Him. It was that in spite of what there was in your heart to condemn you, you had received grace to believe that you had the forgiveness of sins, sonship with God, life, justification, and everything in the atonement of Jesus: that you had access to God by the blood of Jesus, and that this was enough. Absolutely nothing else of any kind was needed. You received peace, therefore, by believing in Christ.

When you begin to have misgivings and there is anxiety and unrest in your heart, what causes it? It is the fact that you again have forgotten what you thought you had learned, namely, that what you must build on is entirely outside of yourself and not within your own heart—that you must build on Christ and His atonement, not on what you feel nor on experiences within your heart. Oh, how slow and sluggish we are to learn that we are not to know anything except Jesus Christ and Him crucified! I think I understand why Jesus so often had to reprove His disciples because they were "so slow of heart to believe," for this is something which I know from my own experience.

At the time the sinner received grace to believe himself saved, he built this faith on the historical fact that nineteen hundred years ago Jesus died for our sins, and on nothing else. Isn't the fact that Jesus has redeemed us just as true when we have no blessed feelings as when we are thrilled through and through with lovely emotions? Of course. Since it is equally true at all times, then surely I can at all times and with the same confidence build the assurance of my salvation and eternal happiness on this truth. My feelings have nothing to do with the matter.

It is on the *Word* that I must build my faith—on the Word which tells of Jesus' finished work of salvation—or else I never shall have firm ground to stand on. Feelings shift and change all the time; the heart is deceitful more than all things, and therefore is not to be depended on. But what God has said stands immovably firm; it is just as true and just as dependable today as yesterday.

It is perilous to build on one's emotions. Those who have not learned to build on the Word, but judge their state of grace by what they feel inwardly—on their feelings—must always have some means of intoxication. Only when they are in a state of emotional intoxication are they happy. Their "edification" consists in having their emotions stirred. As stronger and stronger means are required to stir them up, the case becomes quite difficult; for it is simply impossible to live under high pressure all the time. And when finally no stimulant has the desired effect, such people are "burnt out"; nothing cuts them to the quick, and often the story ends with their saying good-bye to Church and Christianity. They tell how they have tried both and found them to be all humbug.

In Colossians 2:6 is written, "As therefore you received Christ Jesus the Lord, so live in Him." How did we receive Christ Jesus? As poor, unworthy sinners, who had nothing and could do nothing, but who learned from the Word of God that Jesus had redeemed us, and who received grace to understand and believe that this was enough. Then we must also walk in Him. Our condition will never be different so far as this matter is concerned. Just as we are saved by grace, converted by grace, and justified by grace, so we shall have to live by grace, and at last we shall also be permitted to come home to God by grace only, through the redemption which is in Christ Jesus.

> *Prince of Peace, my faith's beginner,*
> *Thou a Savior, I a sinner,*
> *Thou with Amen, I with prayer;*
> *I Thy everlasting debtor,*
> *Thou the One that broke sin's fetter,*
> *Thou God's own anointed heir.*

Therefore we can sing:

> *I build on this foundation,*
> *On Christ, who died for me;*
> *His wounds are my salvation,*
> *My rest eternally.*
> *He is my life eternal,*
> *Me, worthless worm, He'll take,*
> *He is God's Gift supernal,*
> *God loves me for His sake.*

"Thanks be to God for His inexpressible gift" (2 Cor. 9:15).

THOUGHTS OF A CHURCH SCHOOL TEACHER

As we have seen above, our feelings shift and change all the time and cannot be depended upon. We must learn therefore to build on the Word; this alone will provide a foundation that is firm and will not shift beneath us.

As teachers, too, we cannot depend solely upon our feelings. We sometimes grow discouraged. We sometimes fail to see the results of our work. We feel that we don't know enough, and don't really know how to teach what we do know. It is at points like these that we again must turn to the Word.

It is in the Word that we get a fresh view of the students that we teach. There we start to see them in a new perspective. It tells us that they are created by God; they are His children through creation. We see that God created them in His own image, for fellowship with Him. Then the Word shows them to us in their fallenness; we see them rebelling against God. It shows them in need of a Savior. Our feelings about them may vacillate; the picture we see of them through Scripture remains steady. They need a Savior.

However, even as the Word shows us our students, it shows us Christ. It tells us that He has loved them and has redeemed them. We see these students baptized in the Name of the Triune God in accord with Jesus' command. We see that they are sons of God, heirs of His eternal salvation. We see them as members of God's Kingdom, with work to do therein.

As teachers, we would then look at our subject matter. This is not something dry and dull, but is the living Word wherein we see the Living Christ. "The Word of God is living and active, sharper than any two-edged sword, piercing to the division of soul and spirit, of joints and marrow, and discerning the thoughts and intentions of the heart." It is through this Word, and through the Sacraments, that the Holy Spirit operates to bring man to faith in Jesus Christ.

Having seen our pupils and their need for forgiveness, the Christ and His offer of forgiveness, the Word and its assurance of forgiveness, we think of ourselves as teachers and of the task Christ has given us to "go . . . make disciples . . . and teach."

The challenge is a great one, with eternal consequences. We accept this challenge because He dwells in us, and strengthens and guides.

Christian education is possible only because the Holy Spirit is at work. In this we can have faith: that God is at work in the hearts of your students, through His Word, and partly in and through you, the teacher, that "they might have life, and have it abundantly."

Suggestions for Discussion:

1. Do you allow for the expression of feeling in your class?

2. Do you rely too much upon feelings—in yourself?—in your illustrations and explanations to students?—in your expectations from students?

3. Do you help your pupils to see and use God's Word as the basis for their belief and their assurance?

A Case to Consider: Luke 15:22-32, The Prodigal Son